To Betty
Hope you enjoy
the book —
Dr Stan

Business Boot Camp for Women

by

Stan Fine PhD

authorHOUSE®

AuthorHouse™
1663 Liberty Drive, Suite 200
Bloomington, IN 47403
www.authorhouse.com
Phone: 1-800-839-8640

First published by AuthorHouse 2/14/2008

ISBN: 978-1-4343-6153-0 (sc)

Library of Congress Control Number: 2008900521

Printed in the United States of America
Bloomington, Indiana

This book is printed on acid-free paper.

INTRODUCTION AND DEDICATION

For a long time I have seen the need for a general purpose how to book in the small business marketplace. Historically businesses in the startup mode to medium range do not hire marketing managers. In many cases the owner of the company drives the marketing and sales functions. In most cases many of these businesses "shoot from the hip" with gut instinct.

If you are looking for a novel or a fluid chapter to chapter kind of book this is not it. This is a reference book and attempts to provide answers to your marketing questions, how do I do it? And what do I do next?

After teaching women in my classes and consulting with women business owners for the last several years it became apparent to me that a book, like this would help women to start or to grow a business. I hope this book becomes a constant reference companion in your search for answers and success.

Finally I want to dedicate this book to my wife Bethany for her moral support, love and encouragement. Also thanks to the many teachers and professional people that have helped me to make this book what it is.

Special thanks goes to Steve Turner (PR Firm Solomon and Turner) that have added their chapters in this book.

ABOUT THE AUTHOR
STAN FINE

During his 40+ year career, Dr. Fine has become an authority and business consultant on sales and marketing business development issues. His entertaining presentations have made him much in demand as a speaker and seminar leader.

Fine has a BA in Business Administration from Clayton University an MBA in Marketing from Rochville University, and a PHD in Business from Redding University. Dr. Fine teaches at St. Louis Community Colleges School of Continuing Education and has conducted over 200 sales and management seminars at major colleges (Harvard, Drake, Duquesne, and others) throughout the United States for INC Magazine. Some of Stan's credentials are as follows:

As Vice President of Marketing and Sales, Stan spearheaded Connect America's successful market expansion into the long distance marketplace that delivered $2 million in incremental revenues in the 2 years after 5 years of decreasing revenues.

As Director of Marketing, Fine lead XETA Technologies growth, as part of an executive team, from $30 million and 80 employees to $100 million and 400 employees within a three years period.

As Director of Business Development at Grant Thornton Stan built an international consulting practice from inception to $500,000 per year consulting fees and a department of 14 consultants.

As Director of Marketing of a division of General Dynamics spearheaded growth from a $30 million a year 500 employee organization to a $100 million a year 3000 employee organization.

As President of his own consulting firm (World Telecom Associates Inc) Stan grew his business from $90,000 a year to $250,000 within a five year period.

Some of his past additional accomplishments have been:

- Regional Board of Directors American Cancer Society
- Board of Directors Society Telecommunications Consultant
- Board of Directors St. Louis County Juvenile System "Payback"
- Conducted Seminars at Universities for INC Magazine
- United Nations - New York " Seminar Presenter
- Channel 18 – Los Angeles Presenter to the Hospital Satellite
- Spoken on National Public Radio " All Things Considered"

Contributing Authors to Chapters 8 and 9

Steve Turner is Managing Partner of Solomon/Turner, a St. Louis PR firm. He has over 20 years experience in advertising, marketing and public relations. Prior to merging with S. Solomon Associates, an advertising agency, Steve managed The Turner Group. Steve has written many articles on marketing trends on radio and television. His background includes several years in the broadcasting industry including on-air broadcasting, sales management and general management. His areas of expertise include architecture, construction, high-tech, professional services, retail and sports marketing. He is an active member of the Public Relations Society of America, an active member of the Chesterfield Chamber of Commerce and is a former President of the Maryland Heights Chamber of Commerce. He is a graduate of the University of Missouri School of Journalism.

Donna J. Head is a graduate of the University of Kansas. She holds a degree in Broadcast Journalism with an emphasis in News. She has worked as a reporter, anchor and producer for several media outlets. She has developed programs and created formats for several television and radio stations. As a media consultant she has worked with local and national media on special projects and investigations and helped clients develop successful strategies to obtain and maintain partnerships with targeted media outlets. She has created and won awards for her Diversity and Communication Training programs. As a producer she has created several video projects for various educational institutions. She has received additional training from The National Association of Black Journalists and The Radio Television News Director Foundation.

Additional Thanks to **Joel Marion Photography**, 1478 Cherry Creek Lane, St. Louis, MO 63021 for picture on cover of Dr. Fine.

CONTENTS

Chapter 1: How to Sell Like a Pro and Win

Chapter 2: How to be a Good Manager

Chapter 3:
How to Write a Business Plan

Chapter 4:
Successful Trade Shows

Chapter 5:
How to Implement a Seminar Successfully

Chapter 6:
How to Promote Your Business with Little or No Money

Chapter 7:
Internet Marketing

Chapter 8:
How to Master PR

Chapter 9:
TV and Publicity

CHAPTER 1
HOW TO SELL LIKE A PRO AND WIN

Good Rules of Engagement

Far too often, in the heat of the new-account hunt, "rules of engagement" are vague, unstated or—worst of all—assumed. The results are low closing ratios, wasted resources and sales failure. Before investing time and your company's support with any prospect, set fair rules of engagement.

When invited to compete for a prospect's business, salespeople traditionally let the prospect set the rules of engagement. What are those terms? Is the prospect candid and clear about what it takes to earn the business, or does he or she just want a competitive quote? You must know and understand the prospect's rules of engagement before entering the arena.

Better still; develop your own rules before agreeing to compete. What is fair to you? What rules are unacceptable? Don't "wing it" when setting the rules. It's unprofessional to waste your time and the support of your company team without clear, fair, and agreed-upon rules of engagement. Set the rules by asking the following questions:

What's the upfront commitment? By definition, "engagement" means a commitment to something. For example, if you solve a business problem, service problems for your prospect and stay within budget, will you earn the prospect's commitment?

Don't assume this is so until you state this rule of engagement and the prospect agrees. If your prospect doesn't agree, the rules of engagement are not fair to you or your team. Before moving ahead, ask the prospect what it will take to earn his business.

Who's quoting and why? Avoid excess competition. If your prospect accepts bids from multiple salespeople, what does that say about your odds of success? More important, what does that tell you about the perceived value of your professional support? Set agreed-on rules about the mix of competition that's fair to you. When the prospect seeks multiple bidders, ask why before entering the quoting fray. How are your markets assigned? Has one of your competitors ever given a prospect a list of dozens of potential companies in order to block those markets from you? Not only is that unfair to you, but it also puts your competitor's interests ahead of the prospect's. Don't agree to allow other salespeople to block your most competitive markets.

Insist on access to the companies you count on to bring your prospects the best value. That's fair to you and your prospect. Anything less robs you of your tools and reduces your opportunity to succeed.

What's the budget? Understand your buyer's budget before committing to compete. Can your prospect afford you? Is the budget flexible if your solutions add cost? Are service and relationship advantages important, or does the account goes to the lowest bid? Is your sale price within the budget?

Define the decision-making path. What path is the prospect following to reach a buying decision? Who else's input is required? When does the buyer expect your proposal? When can you expect a final decision? Do you have "last look" or the opportunity to adjust your proposal before a final decision is made? If not, does the incumbent or any other salesperson have those opportunities? Is the upfront commitment still valid at decision time? Insist on a fair, logical and clear decision-making path.

Bad Rules of Engagement

Can't you just give me an 'apples- for-apples' quote like everyone else?" When a prospect uses the words "apples for apples," he is saying that price, not value, is the deciding factor. Can you always offer the lowest price? When you deliver a low price, is the incumbent salesperson given a chance to beat, match or split the cost difference? What happens when your service is superior? When prospects control competition by requiring an "apples for apples" quote, run for the hills.

"Would you just bring your best quote so I can present it to the owner?" Once again, no. When an office manager is delegating the task of getting quotes, be careful. If the owner's representative is not the decision-maker, your probability of success is reduced.

Determine your contact's authority level. Can he or she say yes to your proposal? Does your contact have the power to recommend your proposal to the owner, or is his or her task simply to harvest as many competitive quotes as possible? Ask if the incumbent salesperson and any other competitors have direct access to the owner. You must have access to the decision-maker equal to or greater than the incumbent's or any other competitor's.

"Why do you need that?" Prospects must be willing to share information to help you build an effective proposal. Some prospects may not have the information you want. Others might be unwilling to share data they perceive as negative. Perhaps your buyer doesn't trust you with proprietary information such as financial statements. If your prospect can't give you what you need to create a professional proposal or won't provide negative or proprietary information, you're proceeding at your own risk and perhaps preparing to fail in the attempt to gain a new customer.

Create your own rules of engagement before meeting with a prospect, and prepare responses to any of the prospect's rules that are unacceptable. Don't leave your success to chance. When you set the rules of engagement, you present yourself as a professional and become the point of comparison for the competition.

Pareto's Principle - The 80-20 Rule

How the 80/20 rule can help you be more effective

In 1906, Italian economist Vilfredo Pareto created a mathematical formula to describe the unequal distribution of wealth in his country, observing that twenty percent of the people owned eighty percent of the wealth. In the late 1940s, Dr. Joseph M. Juran inaccurately attributed the 80/20 Rule to Pareto, calling it Pareto's Principle. While it may be misnamed, Pareto's Principle or Pareto's Law as it is sometimes called can be a very effective tool to help you manage effectively.

Where It Came From

After Pareto made his observation and created his formula, many others observed similar phenomena in their own areas of expertise. Quality management pioneer, Dr. Joseph Juran, working in the US in the 1930s and 40s, recognized a universal principle he called the "vital few and trivial many" and reduced it to writing.

In an early work, a lack of precision on Juran's part made it appear that he was applying Pareto's observations about economics to a broader body of work. The name Pareto's Principle stuck, probably because it sounded better than Juran's Principle.

As a result, Dr. Juran's observation of the "vital few and trivial many", the principle that 20 percent of something always are responsible for 80 percent of the results, became known as Pareto's Principle or the 80/20 Rule. You can read his own description of the events in the Juran Institute article titled Juran's Non-Pareto Principle.

What It Means

The 80/20 Rule means that in anything a few (20 percent) are vital and many (80 percent) are trivial. In Pareto's case it meant 20 percent of the people owned 80 percent of the wealth. In Juran's initial work he identified 20 percent of the defects causing 80 percent of the problems. Project Managers know that 20 percent of the work (the first 10 percent and the last 10 percent) consume 80 percent of your time and resources. You can apply the 80/20 Rule to almost anything, from the science of management to the physical world.

You know 20 percent of your stock takes up 80 percent of your warehouse space and that 80 percent of your stock comes from 20 percent of your suppliers. Also 80 percent of your sales will come from 20 percent of your sales staff. 20 percent of your staff will cause 80 percent of your problems, but another 20 percent of your staff will provide 80 percent of your production. It works both ways.

How It Can Help You

The value of the Pareto Principle for a manager is that it reminds you to focus on the 20 percent that matters. Of the things you do during your day, only 20 percent really matters. Those 20 percent produce 80 percent of your results. Identify and focus on those things. When the fire drills of the day begin to sap your time, remind yourself of the 20 percent you need to focus on. If something in the schedule has to slip, if something isn't going to get done, make sure it's not part of that 20 percent.

There is a management theory floating around at the moment that proposes to interpret Pareto's Principle in such a way as to produce what is called Superstar Management.

The theory's supporters claim that since 20 percent of your people produce 80 percent of your results you should focus your limited time on managing only that 20 percent, the superstars. The theory is flawed, as we are discussing here, because it overlooks the fact that 80 percent of your time should be spent doing what is really important. Helping the good become better is a better use of your time than helping the great becomes terrific. Apply the Pareto Principle to all you do, but use it wisely.

Manage This Issue

Pareto's Principle, the 80/20 Rule, should serve as a daily reminder to focus 80 percent of your time and energy on the 20 percent of your work that is really important. Don't just "work smart", work smart on the right things.

Ways of Finding Prospects

There are many ways of finding potential targets of opportunity. Below are a few sources you may want to consider when you are searching for opportunities. I always start out thinking of people as suspects first and if and when they qualify I convert them to prospects.

- Current Clients
- Referrals from Clients
- Referrals from Prospects Who said "NO"
- Spheres of Influence
- (Lawyers, vendors, accountants etc)
- Competition (your niche versus theirs)
- Sales Lead Clubs
- Industry Associations Meetings and Directories
- Newspapers, Magazines, Industry Periodicals
- Yellow Pages
- Friends, Acquaintances
- Chamber of Commerce (How to position yourself)
- General Directories
- Cold Calls (Suspects to Prospects to Customer)
- Professional Databases (D&B, Harte Hanks, Info USA etc)
- Direct Mail (ROI formula: ½ of 1% up to 16% with telemarketing)

Cold Letter Marketing

Success or failure depends on a great many things, and there is no way to predict how well cold-letters – first-contact letters to prospects who have probably never heard of you before – will work for you with each prospect over time. Bottom line, how well your cold-letter marketing works is entirely up to you. To achieve maximum prospect response, you must first avoid the 10 most common mistakes that will generate the crumple-and-toss response.

Mistake 1: Allowing Your Prospects To Decide Too Early

How many times have you tossed unopened mail in the trash, because you knew before opening the envelope that it was something you didn't want?

Your prospects are no different from you, so, if your envelope provides enough information for them to make a decision about it, then it may get tossed before being opened. Don't make the mistake of assuming your prospects open every piece of mail they receive.

Mistake 2: Ignoring Your Prospects Time Constraints

Do I really have to tell you that decision-makers avoid letting others waste their time? Must I actually point out that executives spend no more than a few minutes each day going through their mail? Yours is not likely the only letter on the prospect's pile, so at most you have ...

Eight seconds before the decision-maker will make the first yes/no decision about whether to crumple and toss.

It probably took you four seconds to read that last sentence, which has 19 words. So, at most, you have about 40 words with which to deliver your first compelling message, and thereby avoid the crumple-and-toss response. Then again, one compelling point is probably not enough to get your prospect to invest the time to read the entire piece, but a great opening can "buy" you ...

Eight more seconds before the prospect makes his or her second toss/don't-toss choice. That's only 40 more words to make a point so compelling that the prospect will make the conscious decision to read the entire letter.

The second 40 words are probably the most critical of your letter, because they will either cause it to get tossed for good, or "buy" you ...

One additional minute – the average amount of time most decision-makers will invest before making their final crumple and toss decision.

If you don't make your first compelling point in 40 words, your next compelling point in another 40 words and keep your entire letter at 500 words or fewer, your letter won't survive the prospect's three crumple-and-toss decisions.

Mistake 3: Lying To Your Prospects

I once received a cold-letter from a large publishing company, along with a copy of a newsletter it published. The idea was to send me an example of the product the company wanted me to buy, in the hope I'd see enough value to part with some of my money.

Honestly, I never read the newsletter, because after "Dear Gill," the first six words triggered my crumple-and-toss response: "This is not a sales letter."

When I read that, I literally grabbed the entire pile and tossed it straight in the trash (pretty much the same way I delete every e-mail with a subject line that says, "This is not SPAM"). Fortunately, about 10 seconds later, I realized the letter might make a great example of what *not* to do in a cold-letter mailing, so I retrieved it for another look.

In the body of the letter were two attempts to "sell" me on the idea of purchasing a subscription to the enclosed newsletter. In one attempt, the author explained how he thought sending me the free issue was "a smart bet." In the other, he tried social proof by telling me how he figured I would agree with thousands of my colleagues that his newsletter was "a smart investment."

Finally, in the postscript of the letter, the author gave me his e-mail address and asked me to let him know what I thought. (I told him exactly what I thought, and I haven't received a cold-letter since.) If anything in your letter is perceived as a lie by your prospects (and it's their perceptions that count), you may as well save the postage and not send it at all.

Mistake 4: Thinking Your Prospects Give A Hoot About You

How many times have you opened a cold-letter and read the opening sentence, "I'm writing to tell you about my company"? I've been in business for 26 years, and in that time I've received countless cold-letters for accounting services, computer technology services, janitorial services, real estate services, and, yes, even sales consulting services – most of which started exactly that way.

Why in the world should *I* care about *your company*? Isn't it your job to care about mine? Aren't you selling your product or service so something at my company can get better? Isn't your service designed to improve something around here? Who are you to expect me to drop everything I'm doing to learn about your company? If I did that every time a salesperson requested it, I'd never have time to care about mine.

Those are thoughts that flash through my head when I see that subject in a letter. Generally, decision-makers don't give a hoot about you or your company, and offering to tell them about your company will almost always result in crumple and toss.

Mistake 5: Confusing Your Prospects

Industry jargon, acronyms, buzzwords and marketing "super fluff," or anything that is written to impress instead of to prove you can produce a result, will do nothing more than confuse your prospects and result in crumple and toss.

Busy people want to read clear and simple messages, especially when they're opening the mail. Use the writing ability you've developed to keep your cold-letters simple – which is what your prospects want.

Mistake 6: Making False Promises To Your Prospects

Unlike in the legal system, where you're innocent until proven guilty, in cold-letter marketing, you're "guilty" until you prove otherwise. From the moment a prospect opens your letter, he or she will already believe, "This salesperson is going to promise me something he can't deliver."

To avoid the crumple and toss, you must eliminate everything from your letter that the prospect will see as an exaggeration of success, or a promise that can't be met. And remember, it's the prospect's perception that counts, not yours.

Mistake 7: Being Impersonal With Your Prospects

Salespeople often forget that opening a letter and reading a letter are highly personal experiences – both tactile and audible. The recipient feels the weight of the unopened letter, and experiences a rush from tearing it open and risking paper cuts as he or she reaches in to retrieve the contents. (Who among us doesn't enjoy ripping the zip-strip on a FedEx package?) And then there's the anticipation – like opening a box of Cracker Jacks and digging to the bottom for the prize, or opening a birthday card to see how much money with "Dear Executive" or "Dear IT Manager"? Impersonal letters create impersonal is inside.

Granted, these experiences are subtle, but why reverse their positive impacts completely by starting your letter reactions. What could be more impersonal than crumple and toss?

Mistake 8: Sending Your Prospects Poorly Written Material

A copyeditor spent years trying to convince me that high-quality, or polished, writing is more effective than writing containing grammar and punctuation errors. While I understood her message, I maintained that the majority of people wouldn't recognize a grammar mistake if it bit them in the butt, and that even an error or two would not negatively impact results.

Finally, he said, "You're so big on testing stuff; why not test what I'm telling you, so you'll know one way or another?" So I wrote a cold-letter, got it as good as I possibly could and gave it to her to edit. When she was done, and after we agreed to a small wager, we sent 200 letters of my version to one set of prospects and 200 letters of her version to another – making sure there were no real differences in the two groups. The unedited letters produced zero appointments; the copyedited version produced four.

Mistake 9: Failing To Ask Your Prospects For Something

While you can rely on consistent behavioral impulses to help you in certain situations, you must understand that they can hurt you in others.

Think about what prospects actually do as they go through their piles of mail. First, they look for the fun stuff, like checks from customers. Second, they examine anything that seems important, such as a letter from Dewey Chatom and How (just kidding) or go through the items they expected, like the new issues of their favorite magazines. And finally, they work through the pile of uncategorized mail, which is when a pattern that can hurt you begins:

- Open, browse, crumple and toss.
- Open, browse, crumple and toss.
- Open, browse, crumple and toss.

Unless you are lucky enough to have your letter always land on top the pile, where it may get seriously considered, you must be able to overcome the prospect's preconceived notion that your letter is about to waste his or her time. Even if the prospect pauses to read a part of your letter, he or she may already be in a crumple-and-toss rhythm, and may assume yours is "just another sales letter." You must call the prospect to action – ask for something. And, trust me, a final statement like, "If you have any questions, feel free to ask" won't get the job done.

Mistake 10: Forgetting How Your Prospects Read

When you're paging through your pile of mail, reading letters, brochures, postcards and other marketing material, do you read the same way as you would reading a book, or do you scan the material and read whatever catches your eye?

You have two eight-second blocks of time to convince your prospect that the rest of your letter is worth reading. So unless you position your two most compelling points where the prospect will find them while scanning, you can bet your letter will get crumpled and tossed.

The first key to successful cold-letter marketing is avoiding the crumple and toss. So if you want your letter evaluated for the actual content, you must avoid the 10 most common crumple-and-toss mistakes.

The Envelope

The best-written marketing letter will achieve nothing if your prospect fails to open the envelope. So before you consider using cold-letters, you must create a strategy for getting past the initial crumple-and-toss impulse.

When a prospect is rifling through his or her mail and deciding what to open, the decision being made is "Where should I invest my available time?" If you compete for that time by putting your company name, logo, marketing messages, etc, on your envelope, then, when looking at your piece, the prospect is in effect answering the visceral question: "Does this piece of mail *look* more interesting than the others?" Suppose, for instance, that the prospect is opening mail and has 10 pieces that are completely unfamiliar. Further suppose that the prospect typically opens and reads only one third of the mail received.

If you don't want to take the chance of losing the visual-enticement competition, but you still want to send your letters, then your only option is to change the contest itself, so you no longer have competitors. Consider how the prospect's visceral question will change if you put no identifying information – nothing visual – on the envelope at all. Instead of deciding "Does this piece of mail look more interesting than the others," the prospect must decide "Am I capable of tossing this letter without knowing what's inside?" So instead of competing for with nine other envelopes, yours is now in a category by itself.

If you want the odds on your side, put nothing identifiable on the envelope itself – just a plain envelope with the prospect's name, title, company and mailing address, and a return address that contains your name, street, city, state and ZIP.

While there are no silver-bullet answers to most sales puzzles, I think this particular answer comes as close to being a silver-bullet solution as anything ever has, because curiosity is a powerful force.

How Prospects Read

So your envelope was opened, and the prospect is about to read your letter. You have, at most, 40 words you can use to grab the prospect's attention and compel him or her to continue reading. But to be sure you accomplish your goal; you must know which 40 words the prospect is likely to read *first*.

In part, the answer to this question depends on the format of your letter. Since standard business letters are the most common choice, let's examine them.

If you listened to me when I explained that copyediting is a critical component of success in cold-letter writing, you've chosen to use a standard business-letter format that complies with accepted copyediting rules? So, you should have the following in your letter:

Date Line: The date, month and year on which the letter is sent

Inside Address: The prospect's name, title, company name and address

Salutation: An opening greeting like "Dear Joe" or "Dear Mr. Jones"

Message: The text of the letter

Complimentary Closing: A parting phrase such as "Sincerely"

Writer's Identification: Your name and title

Postscript: An afterthought or additional tidbit of information appearing below the writer's identification

Finally I can't predict what percentage of your prospects will respond to only snail-mail because there are far too many variables to consider. I will always have cold-letter marketing as part of my sales system, because:

- It involves creative writing, which I enjoy.
- Once the process is perfected, implementation of the campaign can be easily delegated to someone else, which frees my time for other activities.
- It's the most predictable hunter process I've found.

If you want to achieve success at selling, leverage your speed-writing skills and add cold-letter writing to your marketing activities

Voice Mail Tips

You can use these techniques immediately to dramatically improve your rate of callbacks when you leave voicemail. What you're doing is enabling the recipient with enough detail and reasons so that calling you back just makes good sense.

1. Be brief and get to the point. Don't begin your voicemail with small talk, jokes or other needless filler words. Your message may be one of many, so he may be tired of listening when he gets to yours, so get right down to business. Identify yourself and the purpose of calling.

2. Put the call into context. Say something immediately after your greeting that puts you and your importance in the mind of the listener. She may not remember you if you just met once or twice, so give her a reference. The listener is always thinking, "Who the heck are you and why should I return your call?" If they asked for the call, make sure you say so.

Bad: "Hello Ms. Watson. I'm calling today to let you know of our great new line of..."

Better: "Hi Ms. Watson. This is Karl Walinskas. We met last Tuesday at the Internet trade show in Chicago at my company's booth, The Speaking Connection. I'm following up on your request to..."

3. Give the listener a reason to reply. What does the call recipient get if he gets back to you? Pleasant conversation? A special offer? Offer something compelling that makes the listener want to get back to you for his own good. Everyone wants to know what's in it for me, so provide the listener with an answer to that question.

Bad: "I'd like you to call me back so we can discuss..."

Better: "I'm holding the cruise dates for 24 hours until I hear from you. Call me by tomorrow to book your vacation or plan something else."

4. Time stamp the message. Most voicemail systems have automatic time stamps, but don't rely on them. I never listen to them because the electronic voice is annoying, and many answering machines don't have a time stamp. Let the person know the day and time you called and more importantly, when she can call you back. Provide a window for the return call that is accurate but not too restrictive.

Bad: "We need to talk on the medical account. Call me anytime to discuss."

Better: "I'm calling on Thursday around 3 pm. I can be reached in my office tomorrow from 10 to 1 in the afternoon at 555-1212. Please call to discuss…"

5. Let the listener know how to reach you. Simple right? Give the listener a phone number for a return call and an alternate like a digital phone that's always with you. If you're never around and don't have a mobile phone (like me for years), use the convenience of email technology to let her know an email address that she can reply to that you can be sure to get.

Bad: "Call me back so we can get to it."

Better: "I can be reached at 555-1212 from 3-5 today, or at my mobile number of 555-2121 anytime. You can also get me through email at john.doe@yahoo.com I check it regularly."

6. Provide Instructions. Tell the listener exactly what you want him to do. For business calls, discussion isn't good enough. What is this person needed for? The "I need" phrase is the most powerful two words in the English language, so use it.

Bad: "Call me back so we can discuss the Warren account."

Better: "I need your approval on the final contract to propose to Mr. Warren for the half-million dollar widget order."

7. Explain the consequences of not calling back. This is a great call-return-getter that most people don't use. Think of the cruise example earlier, with the implied consequence of losing the trip reservation unless a return call was made. If you can, be explicit.

Bad: "Honey, call me back about the groceries you wanted me to pick up."

Better: "Honey, call me back to let me know if you wanted skim milk or whole milk. If I don't hear from you, I'll assume you found other nourishment and no longer wish for me to pick up groceries. Bye-bye!"

An additional 12 Tips for Leaving Great Voice Mail Messages

1. Slow Down

Many people leave phone messages as if they were talking to a live person, at the same speed. But it's not the same. Visual cues are absent, the listener may not know your speech patterns, familiar words and phrases are slurred or run together, and the listener can't interrupt to get clarification. And the electronics of the recording device may degrade voice quality.

Tip: When you leave a message on voice mail or answering machine, consciously slow down and pronounce words carefully. As my third grade teacher used to say, "Enunciate."

2. Repeat Your Phone Number

Many callers start by rattling off their name and phone number, then the body of the message, and they hang up. The problem is, as the message taker writes down your name, the phone number flies past. Now they have to replay the message from the beginning. Tip: Always mention your phone number (or fax number or e-mail address) twice, both at the beginning and end of your message.

3. Set the Stage

Prepare the listener before you give a phone or fax number, an e-mail address, or any information you know they'll be writing down.

Tip: Just before you leave that kind of information, start with a lead-in: "My phone number is..." "Here's my e-mail address..." "Our company's address is..." Give the listener time to get mentally ready for what's about to follow.

4. Spell Your Name and Any Unusual Words

Unless you're John Smith or Mary Jones, spell your name after saying it. If your name is unusual, foreign or hard to understand over the phone, it isn't enough to pronounce it clearly. You have to spell it for the listener. Also spell out the names of streets and cities. The same applies to company names. Most people know IBM and Microsoft, but you can't just rattle off a multi-part company name and expect it to be understood. Also, many internet companies' names sound like Alice in Wonderland nonsense when you hear them for the first time. Pronounce names clearly and spell them out.

5. Take Your Accent into Account

Chicago, for example, is a city of many languages, and many individuals speak English with a foreign accent. Accented speech can be hard enough to understand face to face. Over the phone, and filtered through an answering medium, it can be impossible to understand. Accents can even be a problem when you leave a message for someone in a part of the country with a regional speech pattern, like parts of the South or New England.

Tip: If you speak English with an accent, speak extra slowly and carefully when leaving a phone message.

6. Avoid Phone Tag

You call and I'm out. I call you back but you're out. On and on it goes. Phone tag!

Tip: Using e-mail can eliminate the problem altogether, but if you must speak person to person, don't just ask someone to call you. Include in your message a specific time when you'll definitely be in.

7. Say Who the Message is for

A voice mail system may serve more than one person in the same office. Be sure to mention who your message is for. Don't make some poor secretary go from office to office asking, "Is this message for you? Is this message for you?"

8. Plan ahead

Some people, when a machine comes on, freeze like a deer in the headlights, as if they never thought they might get a machine. Then they try to wing it and make up a message off the top of their head. The result is often incomplete and confusing.

Tip: Before you dial your next business call, ask yourself... "What will I say if I get a machine?" Then jot down the key points. Armed with this mini-script, you'll be poised and efficient as you leave your message.

9. Keep it Simple and to the Point

Some phone messages go on and on and on, and the poor message taker is forced to listen to all of it.

Tip: A business message is not the place for free associating or personal chitchat. Stick to business and state your point in as few words as possible.

10. Make a Mistake?

If you misspeak some part of your message, don't just correct yourself on the fly, as you might if you were talking face to face. Start that part of the message over again and repeat it correctly. Don't Say: My address is 786 Southwest-I-mean-east Madison Avenue. Say: My address is 786 Southwest.... Sorry, the correct address is 786 Southeast Madison Avenue.

11. Use a Different Medium for Complex Messages

Try not to leave complicated messages on an answering machine or voice mail. Use a more suitable medium like e-mail, a letter, a phone call, or a face-to-face meeting.

12. Tell Callers How Much Time They Have

And last, a tip directed to the owners of office voice mail and answering machines. There's nothing more frustrating than being cut off in mid-sentence by that damned beep. It means the person has to call back to leave the rest of the message.

Tip: In your greeting message, tell the caller how much time they have. Is it 30 seconds, a minute? Can they leave a message of any length? Isn't that a reasonable business courtesy?

Now, why not tear out this checklist and send a copy to coworkers, staff, and friends. If we all polish our message leaving skills, the wheels of business will turn a little more smoothly.

Acquiring Referrals

Obtaining referrals can be difficult especially if you're not used to asking. But once you've adopted the habit of asking you'll never receive more than enough referrals that it will be hard to follow up on them all. Below are some of the rules of referrals that show why people use referrals to help them acquire sales.

Rules Of Referrals

- 60%-80% of referred leads eventually buy
- Same group buys 23% or more that cold suspects
- Same groups are more likely to refer you to other leads than cold prospects

Referral Introductions (Approaches)

- "Who else do you know that might benefit from our services?
- "What other people need our product that you know?
- "Who else do you recommend who would benefit from these types of savings?"
- "Would you mind contacting (name) to let him know that I will be calling?"

Don't USE!

I will win a sales contest if you buy or support a new house, or send my kids to college, or get a bonus etc.

Cold Calls

The cost of an average sales call visit = $200 so how do you qualify prospects before meeting them and get through the gatekeepers? The main key is to learn how to overcome telephone cold call reluctance. When calling what do you fear?

FEAR OF UNKNOWN - FEAR OF FAILURE - FEAR OF SUCCESS

Ask yourself the question WHAT IS THE WORST THING THAT CAN HAPPEN! They will hang up or they will be condescending or I'll lose my job. Here is another fact. It is hard not to take any returning calls personal. It is critical when you make multiple voice mail calls you remember the person on the other end has a life also. You are not at the top of their list so it may take multiple attempts so don't give up. Also make each voice mail call back message as upbeat as the very first.

DEFROSTING TELEPHONE COLD CALLS – The key here is to have a clear objective before calling. What do you want from the call? An order? An appointment? Write down what you want to accomplish before picking up the phone!

STRATEGIES BEFORE CALLING – What do you know about the prospect? Call the President's secretary to find the best contact for your business and tell her you need help. When you connect with the prospect let them know the President's secretary pointed you in the right direction!

THE CALL - OK here we go! Start With Good morning/afternoon (not hello!). Give your name and the name of the person you are calling: "Good Morning, John Adams with Your Company calling for Bill Jones…(receptionist may say "what company are you with") Answer

"XYZ Company in Any town USA" (stop there!). Remember to be friendly to the receptionist. They are gatekeepers!

THE CONNECTION Avoid "How are you today" and "You don't know me. Ask "Are you in the middle of something urgent?" not "Do you have a minute?" or "Are you in the middle of something important?"

Good way to start! (Person's name + "My name is Bill Jones with (your) company...The purpose of my call is to discuss how we might be able to do business together in the area of ".... Or (Referral Name) suggested I contact you. She thought you would be interested in how we helped her company become more profitable in the area of (name your service you provide)." BE SLIGHT TENATIVE: (I'M SURE WE CAN HELP YOU SOUNDS POMPOUS! Use Maybe, Might or May.

VERIFY THE DECISION MAKER! "I understand that you make decisions about purchasing widgets, is that correct?" If not ask to be transferred to the right person.

EXPLAIN HOW YOU HAVE HELPED OTHERS IN ORDER TO GENERATE INTEREST. This is where you can mention other businesses by name (be careful) or industry and how they have benefited i.e. "We have over 1000 restaurants, similar to yours, that have benefited from our product

GET PERMISSION BEFORE ASKING QUESTIONS. This is so rare you will stand out!

ASK QUESTIONS POLITELY! This is all about finding a prospects HOT BUTTONS when establishing a new relationship. The more you know about a prospect the better your chances. An example question might be "If you could, what would you change about the current supplier?"

How to Design an Effective Cold Calling Script

Who else is in the loop in the decision process? Do you have an effective cold calling script that makes you feel confident when you pick up the phone? Or are you afraid and feeling like your telephone weighs twenty pounds? A key to building confidence and overcoming the fear of the phone is to have an effective cold calling script.

Although there are more effective ways of reaching prospects, the cold call can still make you money if you have the right script. However, having a cold calling script is not the end all. You need to practice your script over and over until it flows off your tongue. You don't want to sound like one of those telemarketers reading the words regardless of what you say.

Cold Calling Script Outline

First you should do your homework and find out who is the decision maker in the company is and ask for them personally when you call. Address them as Mr. or Ms. and their last name. Then give them your name and company and thank them for their time and let them know you will be brief. You should further introduce yourself with a short commercial. One sentence that sums up simply and clearly how you can help them solve a problem.

Next ask them a closing question which further shows the benefits of your product or service.

If you get a positive response, close for the appointment. If you get a no, then you should have another question prepared stating another benefit of your product or service or be direct and ask if the benefit you are offering is important to them?

Let them know that it will be brief. I have many times said to prospects... I need about 10 minutes of your time to show you the benefits of my product or service. At the end of the ten minutes if you believe our product or service is not for you I'll leave. Is that fair? Be prepared with answers to their objections ahead of time.

Sample Cold Calling Script

Good morning Mr. James, My name is Sally Jones with Less-Money.

I appreciate you giving me a moment of your valuable time this morning. I promise to be brief. I specialize in helping trucking companies boost productivity and reduce costs. If I could show you a way to improve productivity and reduce fuel and mobile phone costs, would you be interested? (If you get a yes, close for the appointment.)

I need about 10 minutes of your time to show you the benefits of my product or service. At the end of the ten minutes if you believe our product or service is not for you I'll leave.

Is that fair? Would tomorrow at 10:15 be good or would Wednesday at 2:45 be better? (Then thank them and restate the time and the location of their office.)

Great, I will see you Wednesday the 29th, 2:45 at 2006 Clearwater Avenue.

(If you get a no, ask another benefit question or rephrase your first question)

So, improving productivity and reducing fuel and mobile phone costs isn't important to you? If you feel you may have a good prospect, keep closing, if not hang up and move on to the next. Much of your success in sales will be determined by how much you prepare. This cold calling script is only one of many; however, it will give you a template to use to get started. Get a script that works for you, memorize it and use it to convert more of your calls to appointments.

Close For The Appointment

Close Example:

"It sounds as if our services could be of benefit to you. I'd like to meet with you to find out more about your operation and discuss specifically how we could be of service to your company. Does that sound good to you?"

Set A Specific Time:

Narrow the appointment times don't say, "What time do you have available next week?" (This sounds like you have no appointments)

Say: "I'll be in your area next week. Would you rather meet Tuesday or Thursday? Morning or Afternoon? Two o'clock or three? Finally "Thank the prospect for their time! Reconfirm the date time and street address. Also with the advent of computer software features like Microsoft Outlook I ask for the email address and send them a confirmation via email.

Some Additional Tips To Help You!

- Deepen your voice
- Sound Business like, but not stiff
- Be upbeat and enthusiastic
- Occasionally use the prospect's name
- Show you are listening
- Plan the timing of your calls
- Generally call before sending the prospect anything
- At first, call a new woman prospect "Ms." Rather than Mrs., Miss or her first name
- Avoid calling to confirm your first appointment with a prospect (use email or snail mail to lock it in)
- Decide how many calls you will make is a prospect doesn't return your calls
- Return phone calls
- Always leave your name
- Use a minimum of um's, uh's, ya' know and yeh's
- Don't read a script word for word
- Make it a game so you don't go crazy

For example:

Some life insurance agents celebrate the "no's because statistics show that in their industry for every 24 "no's" there will be a "yes". They tell themselves that each "no" brings them closer to a sale.

Telephone Cold Call Checklist

Here is a list of items to consider before cold calling:

- I strategize before I dialed the phone
- I thought about how I might help this prospect
- I knew my response to the receptionist if he or she asked: "What is this regarding?"
- I consciously deepened my voice tone
- I was upbeat and professional
- I asked qualifying questions
- I avoided giving too much information
- I avoided giving clichés
- I had minimal verbal tricks
- If the prospect was qualified I asked for the appointment

Setting Appointments With The Decision Maker

PREPARATION: *THE KEY TO SALES SUCCESS*

The Importance of Preparation

"The best thing about the future is that
it only comes one day at a time."
-Abraham Lincoln

Even when you have had a "bad "day, week or month, you know that new opportunities are available on your next sales call. In order have the best chance to succeed you must prepare. Preparation for each call is different:

1. Is this a first call?
2. Is this a callback?

Each situation requires its own special plan. This determines your advance time for doing research and preparing for any special needs of your customers or potential customers

Understanding Organizational Needs

Even though "people buy, and organizations don't," however in order to be successful, it is important to be familiar with the basic needs of an organization.

Things You Need To Know!

- You are knowledgeable about business in general.
- You have a basic foundation to think about how your product might benefit their organization
- You have a base of understanding and know the right questions to ask during your sales call
- You feel more confident when you set your appointments and make your presentations

Basic Needs of Any Organizations!

- Make a profit (if what you sell can help make money, increase productivity and /or increase market share, this will be vital to your decision maker.
- Successfully manage and integrate key functional areas of the operation. Success requires knowledge and skill.

Major Business Organizational Units

You need to make sure you understand main functions and departments found in every business operation. History has proven that if you don't understand what motivates each department within a business you will not succeed. Their needs have to become your needs.

Marketing

- Identifies channels of distribution for the products and services
- Who will buy?
- Who can buy?
- Who should buy?

- Who can help distribute?
- What methods can be used?
- Which are most profitable?
- Where should the geographic boundaries end? Or start?

Sales

This is the implementation of the marketing plan.

- Without sales there is no fuel for growth
- In small organizations sales and marketing are often combined
- Salespeople are the front line and the bottom line to a company's success

Resources

- The most valuable assets of any organization are its employees. How they are treated can make or break an organization.
- HR staff need to know about legal issues, benefits, training requirements
- HR staff need to know how to foster an environment that values and supports diversity, recruiting, hiring and retaining employees

Management Information Systems

- This unit controls and coordinates the access of information by both the employees and customers
- Provide 24 hour access and support within a global economy
- Support for all functions within a company as well as the functions to support customers
- Responsible for selecting the hardware and software to meet the needs of an organization

Manufacturing

The group that produces the products or services of the organization.

- Responsible for all aspects of production

- Coordinate with other departments to gather new product ideas
- Design, structure and identify parts/services needed to produce the finished product
- Control the quality and quantity needed to satisfy the needs of both internal and external customers
- Relies heavily on the use of technology for quality control and increased productivity
- If a product is broke or defective this group gets the blame!

Finance

This department is responsible for the monitoring the pulse of the financial health and profitability of the organization.

- They get very little recognition, yet they are heroes on the sideline
- They must support the entire staff's financial needs by providing information, guidance and direction in areas (budgeting, compensation, benefits, costs, revenues etc)
- Ability to keep all departments informed of financial picture (in budget, over budget etc)
- All Tax requirements

Customer Service

The Customer Service Department is a vital link to customers

- Your partner in attracting, retaining and serving customer needs
- Handles irate calls and keeps everyone calm
- Has support Services to enhance the value of the product you sell
- Support services can help secure new business

Understanding The Decision Maker

At this point you need to clear your desk and your mind of everything and anything that might distract you. We are now going to look at one of the most critical elements of a buying decision, one you must never forget not for a minute. People usually buy because of one or more emotional wants and needs. They want their purchase to help satisfy these needs. Take a moment and think about the last thing you bought and why?

Needs of Customers

In order to set appointments successfully you need to understand the need of the customer for a successful outcome. The following are profiles of decision makers and suggested methods for dealing with them:

Ego

Your clues:

- You will hear the clues
- The person will talk about what a great job he or she does for the company
- They stress their value to superiors, subordinates and peers
- They talk about their past, present and anticipated future worth
- They have a lot of pride in their self-worth

Selling Points

- Let them talk
- Don't interrupt
- Compliment them with sincerity on their achievements or value to their company
- Never brag about your own achievements or how successful you are, this will deflate their ego and they won't want to listen
- Always demonstrate how your product or service will support their on-going success

Power

Your clues:

- People desiring power need to be in control
- This person's desk is usually set higher or apart from visitors' chairs.
- He or she may tell you what to do and how to do it
- They become frustrated angry and impatient if things are not done in a certain way
- They have major ego needs and may yell or raise their voice to show you "who's in charge"

Selling Points

- Don't be afraid or intimidated
- Use your power to direct your actions
- Never invade their space
- Do not attempt to get behind their desk
- Sit exactly where they request
- Position yourself as a professional who "serves the needs of decision makers"
- Use Power phrases: "This product can be used in the areas that you think need it most" or "you set the ground rules for action, I'm here to be sure it happens"

Remember to never allow yourself to lose confidence because you feel intimidated of less important. They are only human. The worst that can happen to you is that they say NO.

Profit-Greed

Your clues:

- The person will ask questions such as "How will this help me make money?"
- They will usually ask that question right up front

- Profit and Greed is a strong emotional need based on: performance for shareholders, reorganizational pressures, demands for increased market share.

Selling Points

- Immediately demonstrate statistical success by those who use your products
- Use phrases such as: "increased sales by 30%, reduced waste by 43%, saved $1 million by.
- Don't tell these people how happy your customers are and that you are the leader in your market. THEY DON'T CARE! And it will turn them off.
- Show them bottom-line results
- Be ready with testimonial letters that highlight financial benefits

Survival

Your clues:

- These people often talk about the difficult climate within the organization
- They often say "money is tight"
- They are indecisive
- Their body language is tense – usually leaning forward and talking at a fast pace
- They appear anxious and fidgety
- They are not risk takers and are nervous about making a wrong decision
- They are not in an innovative mind-set

Selling Points

- Offer reinforcement that others in their position have valued, used, and been helped by your service

- Don't tell them your product is new or "leading edge" That will push you out the door
- Show (tell) them how your product has been successful time and time again
- Reassure them that you and your product are proven and reliable

Need to Win

Your clues

- This person is competitive and usually aggressive
- These high energy people are risk takers and use the "ready, fire, aim" method of making a decision
- As "Leaders of the pack" they want success badly
- They are usually very impatient

Selling Points

- Make sure that what you are selling has some competitive benefits to offer
- If allowed by management, quickly highlight three or four top organizations that use your product
- Be sure to point out new or innovative features that will give the customer "leading- edge" opportunities
- Tell them how this person can get to the finish line faster, and if possible, be a starter in their industry

Status

Your clues:

- Titles are important to these people
- They need to know that their supervisors value their contributions
- They will work hard to move up the corporate ladder
- You'll find a lot of workaholics in this area
- They thrive on recognition and accolades for subordinates too

- When you walk into their office you will see diplomas, awards and recognition letters on the wall or they will tell you about their accomplishments

Selling Points

- You need to assure them that what you sell will first help them and then their organization
- Tell them stories about people that used your product and it helped their career to shine
- Describing for them how someone's boss was impressed with the results will fall on receptive ears

Self-Improvement

Your clues

- These people want to do whatever they can to increase their knowledge and effectiveness
- You may see lots of seminar completion certificates on their walls
- You may see several self improvement video courses and books on their shelves

Selling Points

- Find the proper time during your sales call to comment on what you see in their office
- They are proud of their initiatives and want you to notice it
- Be sincere. Ask them about a particular book or course that you see, and what appealed to them
- Describe how your product or service can add to their foundation of knowledge and help increase their productivity

Setting Profitable Appointments with the Decision Maker

A profitable appointment is one that is scheduled with people who can buy or who strongly influence the sale, or a service call to an existing customer.

Planning to set profitable appointments, involves answering 3 questions:

- What is your objective?
- What are the methods you will use?
- What are the benefits to the customer?

What Is Your Objective?

1. To set an appointment with a prospect
2. To set a call back appointment
3. To set an appointment with an existing customer
4. What are some additional objectives?

What Are The Methods You Will Use?

1. Make a list of all prospects that can buy
2. Add at least 50 new names per week
3. Prepare a telephone script!

Scripts That Work And Scripts That Don't And Why

1. Pre qualify your prospects and customers
2. Be sure you are meeting with the decision maker (someone who can influence the sale which may not always be the person signing the deal)
3. Block off time during each week that is devoted solely to scheduling appointments
4. Do not give up your appointment to schedule appointments

What Are The Benefits To The Customer?

Why should a customer schedule an appointment?

You need to establish these benefits before you call

Rules of Appointment Setting

60% of the reason you set appointments successfully is because you choose the best suspects to call - from all your choices. The biggest mistake I see is people doomed to failure because they screwed up before they even picked up the phone. Learn to select the best targets to call, where to find them, and how to get a list. The Importance of setting appointments is crucial to running a business. They are the key to a successful business.

When making appointments try to make your call between one and two minutes maximum. Practice keeping your calls to this time scale, any longer and you could be drawn into a full-scale presentation. It is like trying to describe a musical you have seen but without the music. Remember to create urgency in your call. Tell your contact that you do not have much time but would really like him or her to hear all about your product. Compliment your contact by telling him or her why you have chosen them to hear about your product. Think about this, if someone says something nice about you don't your ears prick up and listen to what is being said.

Leading a conversation with a compliment opens things up for a good reception. But beware of giving forced compliments as people can normally detect them. Before making your call takes a few minutes to think about what information you have on this contact. What special reason is there for sharing this opportunity with them? If the contact is a referral think back to what was said about them and use the positive points as your compliments. **You have now got their attention so you can insert an approach that you find works for you. here are some approaches that you could use:**

Family. Product. Business.

Your approach is entirely up to you. Just remember the object is to get an appointment nothing more. **The last part of your conversation should be to confirm the appoint by:**

Giving your contact choices by setting a time and place

For instance, I'm free tomorrow at (insert time) or we could get together on Wednesday or Thursday at (insert time and place) which suits you? Once you have made the appointment, thank your contact for the time they have given you and reaffirm the date, time and place of the appointment. Write the appointment in your diary or planner. Give yourself a clap for having made an appointment. Now pick up the phone and do it all

Making Effective Sales Presentations

Woody Allen once said "80% of success is showing up," and he was right. Showing up is the easiest way to differentiate you from the competition, because most of them don't. But it's the other 20%, or what happens when you do show up, that's going to determine whether or not you truly will be great.

The Sales Presentation What do the Experts Say

"A good sales presentation starts logically and ends emotionally."
– Zig Ziglar

"Find the customer's key issue, and then concentrate on it."
– Frank Bettger

"Truly outstanding salespeople are excellent listeners."
– Joe Girard

"Remember, you're not selling products or services. You're selling solutions to your customers' problems."
– Robert L. Shook

"Your enthusiasm will be infectious, stimulating and attractive to others. They will love you for it. They will go for you and with you."
– Norman Vincent Peale

"The real salesman must sell something of himself with each sale."
– Robert W. Woodruff

Communicating Your Ideas

"Be fully prepared for your sales call. It's a big confidence booster."
– Ross Perot

"Speak the customer's language."
– Sales Adage

"If you have an important point to make, don't try to be subtle or clever. Use a pile driver. Hit the point once. Then come back and hit it again. Then hit it a third time with a tremendous whack!"
– Winston Churchill

"To get your ideas across, use small words, big ideas, and short sentences."
– John Henry Patterson

"Short words are best and old words when short are best of all."
– Winston Churchill

"It's not what you tell them…it's what they hear."
– Red Auerbach

And Finally

"Remember, you're selling customer benefits, not technology or product features."
– George M. Kahn

"Throughout every presentation, I assume the sale."
– Joe Girard

"Ask yourself this question: Would you buy from you?"
– Zig Ziglar

FACT: 82% of Salespeople Fail to Differentiate

Why is this?

Most salespeople fail to follow a process that matches the natural buying process that nearly all buyers follow. 82% of sellers are out-of-sync with the buyer.

FACT: 99% of Salespeople Fail to Set the Right Call Objectives

Why is this?

This is not surprising since over two-thirds of companies lack a formal sales process. Even fewer have a documented "Best Sales Practices

FACT: 86% of Salespeople Talk too much and Listen Too Little

Why is this?

- Many sales are lost due to the lack of a procedure for presenting product capability. The symptoms associated with poor sales presentation skills include:
- Sales calls that lose momentum
- Customers that lack enthusiasm about your product
- Price or product objections
- Losses to competition
- Stalls such as: "I'd like to think about it."

Effective Sales Presentation Tips

- Be prepared: It's not just the Boy Scout motto; it should also be yours.
- Be concise: Longwinded, stem-winding speeches went out fifty years ago. Your customers want it short, sweet, and simple.
- Be understood: If you want to show how smart you are, write a book. If you want to make a sale, keep it simple.
- Be enthusiastic: If you're not excited about your product, they won't be, either.
- Be descriptive: And when you paint those word pictures, stress customer benefits, not features.
- Be inquisitive: More sales are made with the ears than with the mouth. And remember: the whole point of the sales process is to solve the customer's needs, not your own.
- Be willing to ask for the order: Unless you're willing to extend the customer the courtesy of asking him or her to purchase your product, you're probably wasting your breath.

- Be truthful: Those who over-promise and under-serve are doomed to the economic backwaters of life. But those who under-promise and over-serve are rewarded with fat checkbooks and clear consciences.
- Be yourself: Don't try to be somebody you're not; your presentation should reflect your own personality and style. Besides, if you're pretending to be someone you're not, the customer will know it, probably before you do.
- Be happy or, in the alternative, find another job: Life is short, and if you don't enjoy your work, you'll be sorry. If sales presentations aren't fun for you, you may be in the wrong business. Besides, nobody buys from a miserable salesperson.

Effective Oral Presentations

Speaking effectively is extremely crucial for success in a formal working environment. It has been proven that employees spend more time speaking than writing, whether talking on the phone, conversing informally with colleagues, conducting meetings, or making sales presentations. Research also reveals that the higher an employee moves within an organization, the more important speaking skills become.

This segment focuses only on achieving communication skills relating to sales presentations, including preparing for the presentation, making the presentation with, delivery "do's and don'ts", and incorporating visual aids into the presentation.

Preparation

Preparation for the presentation is almost as important as the delivery of the presentation. In sales you must analyze the selling situation and the audience. You must also determine the goals and objectives of your presentation, choose and shape the content, appropriate communication style, and organize the presentation.

Analyzing the Selling Situation

When analyzing the selling situation you must determine why your presentation is essential. Knowing the situation will help determine the way you shape your content and choose your style. In this analysis you need to ask yourself the following questions:

- What is the need for the presentation?
- What will happen to the organization after the presentation?
- How does the presentation fit into the organization's situation?
- In what surroundings will you make your presentation?
- How does your presentation relate to your audience's actions?
- How can you help the organization?

An example of analyzing the situation would be to conduct background research on the presentation audience to find out what they do, how you can benefit them, and why they asked for your presentation. Analyzing the selling situation can also facilitate answers to other steps in the communication process.

Analyzing the Audience

You need to investigate the personalities of your audience; this will help you determine whether your style should be relaxed and informal or professional and to the point. Questions that can be used in audience analysis include the following:

- How much does my audience know about me and my presentation?
- What does the audience expect from me?
- What is the audience's attitude toward me and my product or service?
- What are the ages and gender of the audience?
- What position does the audience occupy in the organization?
- What is the educational background of the audience?
- What are the political and religious views of the audience?
- What is the audience's personal information (outside-of-work interests)?

Determining the Goal and Objective

Determining the goal and objective of your presentation will help you design your presentation around a specific purpose. Whether you are trying to sell a product, a service, or an idea, you must keep in mind you are also selling your competence and your value to the organization. You must make your purpose evident and relate it to your audience's perspective.

Make sure you state the main point in the beginning of the presentation so that your audience knows what the rest of the presentation will cover. State your objective in one simple sentence. For example, once you have determined your objectives, use the **"T^3" approach**: tell them what you are going to tell them, then tell them, and finally tell them what you told them. If you use this approach you will not digress and your main points will be emphasized.

Choosing and Shaping the Content

Choosing and shaping the content can be very complicated. You want to keep your sales presentation short, interesting, and relevant. Choosing meaningful information that will appeal to your audience and situation is very important. For example, including statistics, testimonials, cases, illustrations, history, and narratives in your presentation can help convey your message.

Choosing the Appropriate Style

Choosing the appropriate presentation style will determine the effectiveness of your content. How you speak can make or break a sales presentation. Questions you need to ask yourself as the presenter include the following:

- What kind of tone do I want to use?
- What kind of image do I want to create?
- What level of language (based on audience analysis) do I use?
- How formal should I be?
- What approach does the audience expect from me?

The most effective style of oral communication is a conversational style because it suggests you are really talking to your audience. This type of communication includes concrete language, short sentences, and a warm and friendly tone. Do not read your presentation to the audience, this sounds impersonal and unnatural. Instead, rehearse what you are going to say because this is crucial for the success of your presentation.

Organizing Your Presentation

Organizing your presentation is the order in which you present your ideas. You must organize your presentation to comply with your audience's needs and perspective. Usually a presentation starts with an introduction that embodies your main point and a preview of what is ahead, the main body of information that supports the main point stated in the introduction, and a conclusion that reiterates and reinforces your main point.

In the introduction grab the audience's attention, and in the conclusion leave the audience with a positive feeling about you and your product, idea, or service. MAKE AN IMPACT! For example, the opening and closing of the presentation are extremely important, so make sure you spend extra time preparing these sections. Include an interesting story or quote that relates to your presentation, it will grab the audience's attention and make your presentation memorable.

Making the Presentation

When you begin your presentation, greet your audience and create a comfortable atmosphere by starting with small talk that is unrelated to your presentation topic. After you feel prepared and comfortable, start you presentation. Stick to the plan for the presentation; tell the audience what you are going to tell them, then tell them, and at the end tell them what you have told them. Do not digress, keep to the time allowed, and when concluding ask if there are any questions. Do not leave your audience with questions; clarify all uncertainties.

Delivery "Do's and Don'ts"

Delivery entails a variety of "do's and don'ts". The following list is some of the most obvious, yet crucial do's and don'ts:

- Do speak clearly (judge the acoustics of the room).
- Don't rush or deliberately talk slow.
- Don't tell jokes.
- Don't speak in monotones (vary speed, pitch, and tone).
- Do maintain eye contact (do not look at only one individual).
- Do keep an eye on audience's body language (watch audience reactions).
- Do keep appearance clean and professional.
- Don't move around too much (i.e., pacing or nervous twitches).
- Don't talk to your visual aids.
- Do be enthusiastic and confident (it will reflect in your presentation).

Some important points to emphasize are your voice (how you say it is as important as what you say), your body language (your body movements express what your attitudes and thoughts really are), and your appearance. The success of a sales presentation relies heavily on your delivery style. All the preparation work can go smoothly, but if you do not deliver your presentation with confidence, enjoyment, assertiveness, and enthusiasm, then all the preparation is worthless.

Visual Aids

Visual aids, if used correctly, can enhance interest in a presentation. Effective communication is both visual and verbal.

Conclusion

By following the outlined steps and lots of practice, you can acquire effective oral communication skills for making sales presentations. Effective communication is important for a successful career in business.

Additional Tips for Successful Presentations

Feeling some nervousness before giving a speech is natural and healthy. It shows you care about doing well. But, too much nervousness can be detrimental. Here's how you can control your nervousness and make effective, memorable presentations:

Know the room. Be familiar with the place in which you will speak. Arrive early, walk around the speaking area and practice using the microphone and any visual aids.

Know the audience. Greet some of the audience as they arrive. It's easier to speak to a group of friends than to a group of strangers.

Know your material. If you're not familiar with your material or are uncomfortable with it, your nervousness will increase. Practice your speech and revise it if necessary.

Relax. Ease tension by doing exercises.

Visualize yourself giving your speech. Imagine yourself speaking, your voice loud, clear, and assured. When you visualize yourself as successful, you will be successful.

Realize that people want you to succeed. Audiences want you to be interesting, stimulating, informative, and entertaining. They don't want you to fail.

Don't apologize. If you mention your nervousness or apologize for any problems you think you have with your speech, you may be calling the audience's attention to something they hadn't noticed. Keep silent.

Concentrate on the message -- not the medium. Focus your attention away from your own anxieties, and outwardly toward your message and your audience. Your nervousness will dissipate.

Turn nervousness into positive energy. Harness your nervous energy and transform it into vitality and enthusiasm.

Gain experience. Experience builds confidence, which is the key to effective speaking.

The Sales Call

Breaking the ice is often the critical starting point for the success of your meeting. Your goal for the beginning of the call is to have the customer:

- Be comfortable with you
- Want to listen to you
- Value what you have to say

You are the director of your own first impressions. The first decisions you want the customer to make are:

- You are a professional – in image, knowledge and communication skills
- You have the customer's best interest in mind
- You are enthusiastic and believe in the benefits of what you are selling

Tips to help you begin

Greet your customer by name – and get it right! Everyone loves to hear their own name, but not when it is mispronounced

Show respect for every person you meet. Respect is a universal sign of goodwill

Be informed and sensitive to the needs of cultural environments different from yours

Tell the customer what you would like to accomplish during your time together. Be sure to tie it in with an advantage for them.

Sample Script

Mr./Ms Prospect, I appreciate the opportunity to meet with you today. As I indicated on the phone, my company has a product/service that I believe will have benefit to you and your company. In order to maximize our time together, I would like to explain the mission of my company and how we serve our customers.

Then, I would like to understand what is important to you, your priorities for (type of product or service) and how our product might be of benefit to you. Would this be Okay?" *Sometimes small talk before you begin is ok.*

In order to make a sale you must know what your potential customer needs:

- Sounds simple maybe not
- Some customers know and will tell you
- Sometimes they know and are not sure how to get there
- Other times the just don't know

It is imperative that you are given enough time.

- Don't rush the presentation
- If your customer has an emergency or needs to cut the meeting short reschedule right then and there.

Sample Script to Use

"Mr. Customer, I'm sorry that we have to cut it short. I understand. I'd like to reschedule our time together to be sure that we discuss your specific needs. Then I will be able to give you all the specific information that targets what you want. How is (day) at (time) or would (day) and (time) be better?

Do not rush. Many salespeople have a tendency to rush if they are being rushed. If you do this, most likely you won't make the sale.

A Method to Discover Wants and Needs

I want to make it clear that this is one of hundreds of techniques. The ultimate key is to get the prospect to identify their pain points and what their return on investment will be if you take care of their needs.

Although basic, it is the technique that I am going for (e.g. fact finding). So here it is:

- Use a Prepared Priority Sheet of information you want to get
- Let your prospect know that you have prepared it just for him or her
- Take out a customer profile so the customer will know you have done some preliminary work about their company
- Share your initial data and ask the customer to expand

Example of a dialogue on the above

"Mr. Prospect, in my visits with many (CEO's CFO's, etc.) they have shared their current and anticipated priorities. In order to maximize our time together, I would like to focus on what is important to you. Is that okay with you? (Now take out Priority Sheet).

"I would appreciate it if we could identify all areas of priority that are important to you. Sometimes a prospect will say "They are all important" you respond "I am sure they are. Which ones take up the most time? Then offer your pen.

Be Quiet and Let Them Fill It Out

This is the first tangible way to identify top priorities. When the customer is done ask them to identify and circle the top three.

At this point you can begin to ask at least 2 open-ended questions:

- Of all the areas why is (state 1) most important right now?
- What would help make it happen?
- When do you think this could be accomplished
- To achieve this goal, what do you feel would make the biggest impact right now?

Finally, before you end your needs analysis, uncover a long-term (1 year or more) question. Here you can identify the vision and dreams of your customers. "(Name of Customer) let's say its one year from now. You're sitting back in your chair and you say, I did it – I accomplished it. What did you do?" BE TOTALLY QUIET AND LISTEN!

Confirming Your Customer Wants and Needs

"OK! You have just completed your needs analysis and are feeling confident. You have done a great job asking questions." Let's start focusing on what to do next? Are you thinking?

- I hope I can get done in time?
- I'll show her the "hot" new products
- I need more sales to meet my quota!
- I've got to sell something! If you are thinking as above you are missing the target. You got your first yes then the prospect agreed to give you information. You need to summarize and now go back for YES #2

Prospects usually do not object to hearing you repeat their Wants and Needs. In fact it helps to solidify their sense of importance

Script Validation

"Mr./Ms Prospect before I review the products/services that my company offers I want to be sure that I understand exactly what is important to you. Based on that understanding, I will provide you with specific information and ideas on how our products can work for you. Would that be all right?"

So if my products will meet your needs and objectives would you give serious consideration to doing business with us?

My further recommendation is to send an email or letter to the prospect restating your findings which they agreed to. The next time you meet these findings must be in your proposal with the solutions.

Proposals

Once you have found the prospects hot buttons (pain points) you will need to develop a proposal. Here are a few guidelines for your proposal development.

Focus on the customer's hot buttons. A proposal should focus on how your product or service will help prospects achieve their goals and meet their objectives. Although you may have a standard template you usually use, each proposal should be individualized to meet the particular prospect's needs.

Keep it as short as possible. There are times--especially when technical statistics and complicated products are involved--when proposals need to be packed with data. Otherwise, you should keep the proposal as short as possible while still making sure it contains all the necessary information. Proposals that have gorgeous covers include press releases and a dozen testimonial letters may look good, but the truth is that 99 percent of the time, the prospect will flip through all those pages and go right to the dollars, and you end up selling on price instead of value. Focus instead on what the client really wants to know.

Ask the prospect how to write the proposal. Say this: "If you were to get the proposal right now, what would be the three most important points that would help you make a buying decision?" Have the prospect prioritize those points, and then construct your proposal accordingly. If the prospect has formal proposal requirements, ask whether he or she has written guidelines you can follow or even a previous proposal you can review to make sure yours fits within the proper parameters.

Think of your proposal as a tool to forge a strong and long-lasting relationship with this prospect. Focus on what the prospect sells and how you can help him or her achieve those goals. When prospects see that you've put in the time and effort to understand their business and objectives, your proposal is sure to end up making the sale.

Presentations - Great Go For It!

OK you are now in the presentation meeting so here is how I recommend you proceed.

Script: Create the awareness of a Problem and or Need

"Ms. Customer, in our last meeting you indicated that (repeat the priorities) are important in meeting your objectives. I would like to focus on showing you how our (name of your product/service) will help make that happen." **Demonstrate and confirm that you can help the customer:**

- Paint a picture with words before actually showing your product (i.e. describe its purpose)
- Explain how your products or services fill a need.
- Describe the product, how it works and the benefits to the customer. This shows the customer the solution provided by the product – the payoff (WIFM)

You need to effectively isolate and demonstrate each product to show off its clear value to the customer. Don't show everything you've got all at once. The customer may feel overwhelmed or become confused. A confused mind doesn't buy.

Finally: Remember to isolate each product during the presentation, link it to its benefits and get confirmation as you go along!

Closing The Sale

Recognizing Buying Signals

- A Professional Salesperson pays attention to customers to determine when they are ready to buy
- Answering questions gets you one step closer to the sale
- Use your ears. Sometimes customers ask questions or make statements that signal that they are ready to buy

- Use your eyes – sometimes it's not what they say but what they do (i.e. start ready the contract you just placed in front of them)
- Be enthusiastic about what you are selling. Customers can tell if a salesperson is bored or disinterested

The Rules of Closing

- A Close is really a beginning. It is the start of an ongoing relationship.
- Even if you sell something the prospect won't need again for several years (like a house) you still want to keep in contact with your buyers. (Special point: happy customers provide referrals)
- If the proposal presentation has gone well and your prospect seems interested, start closing the sale.
- Too many salespeople don't initiate a close. Instead they say "Why don't you think about it? Or I'll leave this brochure. Call me when you've decided." They leave the business on the table for a competitor to take.

Oh-OH… (When a customer has second thoughts) ouch!

That uneasy feeling – the customer begins to waffle what do you do?

- "My business associates told me about a competitive product that does more"
- "The vendor down the street offers the same product for 25% less"

Your job is to help the customer get past the uneasy feeling by:

- Provide reassurance about the product or selection
- Most important don't force the sale
- You may be able to offer other solutions depending on the nature of your business (e.g. a trial period, or 90 day warranty with money back or try service at 1st at your expense for "x" days

or try product for 6 months and if not satisfied we will help you purchase a new product and withdraw ours)

- STOP! At this point since this is such a critical component of closing the sale. Remember we have all been there and have had our hearts drop because of this type of situation.

The Objection Handling Process

Keep Calm

- Sit back; make sure your body language reflects relaxation,
- Don't lean forward or cross your arms...keep quiet.
- Your prospect may be expecting a rebuttal or a "but" from you, but it is NOT going to happen.

Let the customer talk

- Allow the customer to say anything and everything he/she wants.
- Do not interrupt
- Listen and listen some more
- Do not from any judgments or start thinking about a rebuttal
- Wait until the customer has finished

Acknowledge What the Customer Said

- Make a sincere statement, a simple concession
- The customer may be expecting you to challenge. DON'T
- Example response "Many customers initially felt this way. I can understand what you are saying" or "If I were in your shoes, I could see why this would be important" (this helps relax the prospect)
- If their objection seems misguided, don't reveal that you think so.

Ask for Clarification

- Ask some open ended questions that start with what, why, where, when, who and how

- Get the prospect to talk
- You want to understand and identify what the barrier is
- Do not attack in voice or body language
- They need to feel comfortable with the process
- Ask a question about the specific objection "Mr. /Ms Prospect I want to understand what is important to you. "What will be important to make this work?" or Why do you feel your employees wouldn't use it?" or Why would it be best to come back in 6 months?"
- Based on their answer ask at least one more question to ensure that you understand what's keeping you from a sale.

Confirm what you just heard

- Repeat what your customer has just told you.
- Use the same kind of words
- Don't add or delete anything-just restate it
- You want to show that you listened
- This confirmation is your pathway to the sale because you will find out if the prospect did not see how they would benefit or make money

Conclude and Close

- Start asking closing questions
- "If I could show you how you would increase your market share by using this product would you be inclined to give it a try?"
- "Is there anything else that would prevent us from doing business?"
- If you get a YES to the 1st question and a NO to the second question begin representing your product, and once again align it with the information gathered during your needs analysis.
- Keep it simple and benefit oriented
- You should be closer to your sale

Turn Objections Into Sales

Objections can be one of the most frustrating parts of the sales process.

OR

You can turn it into a way of identifying why your potential customer is not buying.

The true sale masters have learned the art of handling objections such as:

- There is no money left in the budget
- It costs too much
- I want to think it over
- I want to discuss it with
- We already have a similar program
- Maybe in a few months or next year
- I really don't need it
- I'm too busy now to decide
- We're different

There Are 2 Reasons Why Customers Usually Object:

- They are not convinced that they will personally benefit
- They don't see how their organization will get a return on their investment

The Difference Between Objections And Stalls

- Objections: Product related reasons for not buying (e.g. too expensive)
- Stalls: These are not product related (e.g. Call me back after Christmas)

Action To Take!

- Uncover the real reason for not buying (a stall is not a real reason)

- Isolate each objection and stall, and handle them one at a time
- "You must handle each objection or stall one by one. Don't try to handle them all at once. You'll lose."
- "Mr./Ms. Customer, I'd like to address each of these areas, because obviously they are very important to you"
- If you don't do this the customer will become defensive

Close With A Service Orientated Approach

Let's separate you from slick "sell 'em and leave 'em salespeople."

Consultative sellers always let the customer know, before walking out the door, what to expect from them.

Consultative Salespeople:

- Sell their product or service and continue a relationship that began on trust
- Provide ongoing service to help support continuous success

Before you walk out the door you want to ensure 3 things:

- You understand the needs of your customer
- Your customer understands the value and benefits of your products
- Your customer knows how you will continue to service his or her account

Your professionalism is the mark you leave

"Ms. Customer I appreciate the time that we've spent together. You have identified the areas of major importance to you, and I will keep your list of priorities in your account file. As we continue to work together, I will update this list as your needs change. I want to ensure that our on-going relationship always targets the areas that are most important to you."

"My goal is to be of continuous service to you. Yes, I am happy that we are going to do business together, but it does not stop here. I want you to always be my customer, so here is how I will follow up. I will call you in 30 days to make sure everything is working well for you. Then I will call you every (name and interval that make sense, never more than 3 months) to keep track of any changing needs or priorities, As needed, I will schedule appointments to review your current situation and recommend new products or service initiatives. How does this sound to you?

No Sale Today

Let's say that you don't make the sale.

- Don't walk out in a huff or show frustration
- You still want another chance
- Don't forget the final image you leave with your customer will usually be the impression of you that remains with them.
- If you have a call back opportunity based on specific circumstances, set the appointment before you walk out the door.

Additional Objection Handling Techniques

In my humble opinion many sales are lost because the salesperson had not yet overcome the objections presented by the prospect. Try to remember this, a prospect presents an objection because they are uncomfortable with the information you have presented and want you to make them feel that it is the right decision. You may be surprised how little you may have to do to push the decision in your direction. In addition to the above strategies, here are some additional objection handling techniques to help you along:

Boomerang method

Technique

- When people object, turn them around by using what they say to prove that they are wrong. Use their own arguments like a boomerang, so they go around in a circle and come back to persuade them.

Examples

- Yes, it is expensive, but I don't think you would want to buy your wife a cheap present.
- Indeed, the house does need work, but as you said, you are very good at Do-It-Yourself work.
- Certainly, if you do not have the money today then we can arrange it all for tomorrow.

How it works

- By using what they say, you are saying that they are right. And when you attach what you want to what they say, then by association, what you want is right.

Objection Chunking

Technique

- You can take a higher, more general viewpoint or a more detailed focus.
- Chunking up (also called Helicoptering) lets you see more and understand the big picture. When you chunk up, specific issues seem small and insignificant. My worries about a scratch on a car are nothing in comparison with world peace.
- You can expand the pie, showing them how they are getting not only the basic product, but other things as well. You can add widgets and warranties. You can add emotions like the added peace of mind they will have from your product.
- Chunking down drills into the detail, highlighting and addressing significant concerns. It also distracts attention away from more difficult concerns in other areas. You can reduce the apparent size of the objection, for example by changing a dislike of town into a dislike of a neighborhood or just a street.

Examples

- Let's look at the big picture. What do you really want achieve by using this?

- That's interesting. Tell me more about that... How does your CEO think about this?
- Tell you what. Let's get one of your engineers to consider the situation.

How it works

- Taking a different perspective has a dual effect, first of reframing to create a different attention and a new understanding, and secondly of distracting from what might be a difficult.

Conditional Close

Technique

- When the other person offers an objection, make it a condition of resolving their objection that they make the purchase. You can also use this approach to make any trade - for example if you want them to watch a promotional video, offer a cup of coffee.
- Always, by the way, phrase it in the form 'If I...will you...' rather than 'Will you...if I... This is because our brains work very quickly and starting with 'will you' causes them to begin thinking immediately about objections and they may miss the exchange. On the other hand, starting with 'If I...' will cause psychological closure on what you are offering thus drawing them in to the close.

Examples

- You say you want a red one. If I can phone up and get you one, will you take it today? If we can figure out the finance for you, will you choose this one?
- If I get you a cup of coffee, would you like to sit down and look through the brochure?

How it works

- The Conditional Close uses the Exchange principle to build a social agreement that if I solve your problem, you will buy the product in return.

Curiosity

Technique

- When they declare that they do not want to buy from you, act curious.
- Do not just ask 'Why??', but express a curious interest that says 'how interesting - I wonder why'. Getting the objection out before they leave then gives you one last shot to keep them there. Even if they still leave, it also lets you know why you failed to sell to them today and so improve your sales skills.

Examples

- I know you don't want to buy this, but before you go, could you just let me know what your reason was? I was just wondering what led to your decision not to buy this today. Most people really go for this one. I am a little curious as to how you decided otherwise. Did I not explain it clearly enough? Was I a bit too enthusiastic? Sorry, but I just love these.

How it works

- Being curious appeals in part to their child-self, whereby you say 'Wow, isn't that interesting!' and invite them to a game of exploration and discovery. Curiosity also evokes their need for novelty in their life. When you are non-threatening and not in 'closing mode' they may well relent and give you the information you need.

Deflection

Technique

- Avoid handling an objection by deflecting it such that it does not hold up the proceedings. Listen to it. Show understanding of the concerns. Then carry on as if nothing had happened. Say that you will come back to it later. Maybe you won't have to. Give an excuse, such as not having information or having to talk to somebody else later.

Examples

- Yes, I see what you mean...mmm...Now let me show you the range of finishes you can have...Good point. Can I come back to that later?...thanks...Now what I was saying was...Yes, I've got some information about that back at the office somewhere. Can we carry on now?

How it works

- By accepting their objection you are accepting them as a person, and the additional harmony and rapport created may be enough to overcome the objection. Refusing to answer their objections now may also be a power play, where you are demonstrating authority and control over the situation. If you can get away with it, they may cede more power to you.

Feel, felt, found

Technique

- First empathize with them, telling them that you understand how they feel.
- Then tell them about somebody who felt the same way.
- Then tell them how that other person found that things were not so bad and that when they did what you want the buyer to do they found that it was actually a very good thing to do.

Examples

- I understand how you feel about that. Many others have felt the same way. And what they have found is that.... I know how you feel that it looks rough. I had a person in here yesterday who felt the same when they first looked at it. But when they tried it on they found that it was so comfortable. You know I feel the same about products when I first see them. I felt the same recently when I bought a new car. But when I took it home for the weekend, I found that everyone who saw it was so envious.

How it works

- By empathizing with how they feel, you are building harmony with them to create rapport. When you talk about how somebody else felt, you move the focus to a more objective place which they are likely to trust more. This also makes them a part of a group such that they do not feel alone. When they are attached to that group, then you move the whole group by telling how the person in the group changed their mind. The buyer, being attached to the group, should change their mind at the same time.

Handling objections with humor

Technique

- When they object, do not respond with negative emotions such as anger or frustration. Defuse the tension with gentle humor, maybe feigning shock or otherwise poking fun at yourself. Be careful about making them the object of humor. It can be done, but you need to be sure first that they will not be offended.

Examples

- Oh no! What will we do? (smiling)
- Well I think this car would be very sad to see you go home without it.
- I think I've lost my touch. (Looking at hands with puzzled expression)

How it works

- When you receive objections it can be very frustrating and it is very easy for these emotions to leak out. By reframing the situation with gentle humor, you can show that you are not offended by their refusal. Remember that they too may find objecting embarrassing and uncomfortable, with the result that they may well want to get away from you (and the embarrassment) as soon as possible.

Justification

Technique

- Rather than fight the objection, justify why it is reasonable. Tell them how you have deliberately made what you are selling this way for a particular reason.

- If they complain about price, tell them the product is built for a superior market.
- If they complain about quality, tell them that this is to allow you to charge a very low price.

Examples

- Yes, the car is expensive, but it is a rare import and cost a lot to bring over here.
- I know it is not new, but it will give your image depth, making you look more established. It is large, which is why most people who buy it find that visitors notice it at once.

How it works

- When people object, they often are saying that what you are offering is somehow unfair or wrong. If you can subsequently show that it is fair and reasonable, then they no longer have reason to object.

LAARC

This is another acronym to help you remember things to do when you are handling objections from your customer.

Listen

- First listen to what they have to say. Avoid the temptation to jump in at the first moment you can. Wait patiently for them to complete what they are saying.

Acknowledge

- When you have heard them, acknowledge the person, their right to object, the validity of their objection. If you do not do this, they may take your response personally and the conversation will descend into a failing duel.

Assess

- Having listened to and acknowledged the person, assess the situation. This may mean asking various questions to probe for further detail. You know when you have completed the assessment stage when you can fully empathize with the person's objection.

Respond

- Only when you have a proper grasp of the objection should you start to respond. Structure this carefully, perhaps using one of the objection-handling techniques here. Always be careful to ensure you respond fully and adequately to the objections given. Beware of straying off the path of responding to the objection or else you may end up creating more objections.

Confirm

- Finally, check with the other person that they have understood your response and that it addresses their concerns. If the other person still has the objection, repeat the loop. See if you have listened well enough in the first place. Check that you have assessed their situation correctly. Ensure that the response fully and adequately addresses their concerns.

LAIR

This is a simple objection-handling method for getting the sale.

Listen

- First listen to them, hearing their concerns and objections. In doing this, listen closely to their real needs and how important things are to them.

Acknowledge

- Echo back what you heard to show that you understand and to get the other person to elaborate further to give you the full details of their objection.

Identify the objection

- Identify the objection and check that they agree that this is their only reason for not buying. Possibly set up a Concession Close so that if you can handle the objection you will get the sale.

Reverse the objection

- Turn around the objection. Use "yes, but" or other methods to show how the truth is in fact the reverse of what was being objected to.

Objection Writing

Technique

- When they object, tip the bucket to get all remaining objections, writing these down as you go on a clean page of paper. Then show it to the other person and verify that if you address these, then there are no reasons for them not to buy.
- Then, as you handle each one, cross it out. You can ask the person before this "So, we have addressed this. Can I cross this out now?" A variant of this is to summarize the objections into one word or a short phrase. Thus you write down price, size and so on. This allows you to reframe slightly what they are saying.

How it works

- Writing things down is useful for a visual thinker. It also moved the problem onto the external, objective sheet of paper (from their subjective thinking). And then it allows you to cross it out. The act of crossing it out causes closure, on eliminating the objection.

Pre-empting objections

Technique

- Tell them about a possible objection before they object. Then handle the objection so it cannot be brought up again. Make the objection rather weak and the handling rather strong. Tell them stories of other people who objected and then looked foolish.

Examples

- I had one person that didn't like the shade, but then they had not realized that this was the latest fashion. You might find this expensive, but we can find the right deal.

How it works

- If you answer the objection before they bring it out, then they are unable to voice the objection without appearing to not have heard you.

Pushback

Technique

- Do not accept the objection. Push back assertively (not aggressively). Object to their objection. If they are wrong, tell them. If you think they are not being truthful, show that you know this. You can push back either directly, by telling them they are wrong, or indirectly, by showing them that they are mistaken. Indirect pushback is usually likely to reduce further objections, unless you have concluded that a 'short, sharp shock' is likely to be more effective.

Examples

- That's not right. This product is the cheapest on the market. I can see that you might think that. But the latest survey has shown that we are the lowest cost supplier.
- Would you like to check those figures again? I think you'll find they are not accurate. Good try. But I can see that you can afford more than that.

How it works

- A direct response to an objection can be a shock that the other person will accept.
- Exposure of a trick puts the other person on the defensive and may well make them want to compensate you for their deception.

Objection Reframe

Technique

- When they object, reframe their objection as something other than a 'no' so you can continue with your selling. Reframing the objection as a misunderstanding (and take the blame for this yourself). Reframing the objection by taking the subject and turning it around. Reframe a small difference as being the critical difference. Reframe 'required specific experience' to 'relevant experience'.

Examples

- I can see that this is not making sense. Sorry - let me put it another way.
- The cost may be high, but the cost of inaction may be higher. Yes, blue is an unusual color. It will make you look really original.

How it works

- Reframing uses what the other person has given you, which makes it more difficult for them to deny it.

Objection Renaming

Technique

- A simple approach to handling objections is to change something in what you are presenting. Some examples are given below, but you can think of more, of course.
- Objections have names. It may be price, worry or something even more specific. Turn price into cost of ownership. Turn worry into reasonable concern.
- Words have very individual meaning, which means that changing 'heavy' into 'weighty' or 'strong' into 'powerful' can change the meaning of a whole sentence.
- Renaming the objection changes it. Or should I say 'putting the problem into new words creates a whole new world.'

Examples

- You say you are worried and I can see you are concerned and that tells me you are interested in good quality products. When you consider about how long it takes, you may also think about the free time it will give you. You said you would talk to your partners. Could you think instead of discussing it with him?

How it works

- Words are 'little packets of meaning' and can have complex schema associated with them, as the deeper aspects of linguistics show. Changing just a word changes the meaning of what is being discussed, looking at it in a different light.

Reprioritize objections

Technique

- When they have a priority which is stopping them from buying from you, find ways of changing the priority. Explore the criteria they are using to decide. Probe to find how important each criterion is. Appeal to their values, which include a system of prioritization. Reframe their arguments so they naturally change priority.
- At the same time or alternatively, increase other priorities that will lead to them buying from you.

Examples

- You are very loyal to your current supplier, but should you be more loyal to your family? You are right, price is important. But how much more important is quality to you? A big picture would look nice, but with smaller pictures you can show more of them.

How it works

- When evaluating between different choices, we use different criteria and different weighting of those criteria. We also get fixated on particular solutions and forget about other criteria. If you can change criteria, change weights or remind the other person of forgotten criteria then you can get them to reprioritize.

CHAPTER 2
HOW TO BE A GOOD MANAGER

What is Management?

Management is the employment of human, physical, and financial resources to achieve organizational goals. Managers are the people who conduct these processes. Management focuses on the results of teamwork rather than individual efforts. It is the job of the manager is to coordinate the work of others. The Manager is held accountable for their work.

The five main jobs of managers are planning, organizing, staffing, leading and motivating the organization, coordinating through communication of objectives and plans, and assessing and measuring the work of employees.

Effective managers are able to use their skills in each of these areas to attain the goals of the organization. Though it is impossible to be "perfect" in every one of these areas of management, good managers are usually very strong in most of them and use delegation to shore up their weaknesses in others. Management can be a science but is also an art. The manager who can balance their people skills with the ability to plan. Organize, and make assessments will be successful in the long run.

Being A Good Manager

Being a good manager is not only about getting your job done, but more importantly, earning the respect of your team. Some thoughts, based on personal experience:

Stop thinking of yourself as a 'Boss' - whether you are the manager or not, you are first and foremost a part of the team. Don't alienate yourself by sitting in a high chair. Nobody likes a windbag.

Lead by example - I always think that to be a good manager, you need to understand what your team is doing. Even if you are not 'hands-on', you need to earn the respect of the team and make them believe that you have an overall guiding vision of what the team is working on. If not, you will end up, at best, being a resource manager.

Learn to Delegate - one of the hardest things for new managers is to delegate to and trust other team members. Typically, when a good engineer steps into the shoes of a manager, he still wants to do everything on his own - don't fall into this trap. If you do not delegate responsibility to your team, your team members will feel stifled and will not be able to grow. And delegation is one of the hardest things a good manager needs to learn to do well. It involves trust and the ability to succeed without micro-managing

Never micro-manage. No one likes being micro-managed. One of the things you will learn, as a new manager, is that when people are given a responsibility, most of them rise to the challenge. Give them a chance. Step back, keep a track of the overall goal but don't walk up to your team members every half hour asking what is going on.

Be careful of overprotection - As a manager, it is critical for you to take care of your team, which includes shielding them from harsh criticisms from others in the organization. However, be very careful of over protection. A good manager will always balance protection with positive criticism to ensure that the team also knows their shortcomings so that they can improve. It is your responsibility to make sure that your team is on the path to constant personal improvement. The worst thing you can do is keep them under the impression that they are the 'best' and have them ignore areas of improvement.

Plan milestones for your team members well in advance (typically a year at least) - so that you can track their progress concretely through the year. Your team deserves to know how they performed objectively.

Take performance reviews seriously - In a typical corporation, the rise of your team largely depends on the reviews that you propagate to the upper management. A review should be timely and as objective as possible. If you have a problem with a team member, step back and determine if it's a problem with the team member or with you. If it is the former, before you put it in the review, consider if it is one-off, due to special circumstances or a repeatable problem that needs to be corrected.

Give an opportunity for your team to give you input on what they think of you. Most importantly, act on their feedback. Being a manager does not always make you right. Don't let your ego get into the way - learning is a 2 way process, from you to the team and from the team to you. Self improvement is key for you to improve as a manager and a leader.

All work and no play... - Don't get too tied in with 'deliverables' and 'schedule'. Make some time to take your team out for a lunch or a party.

Challenge your team - once in a while push your team to achieve more than they think they are comfortable doing. Sometimes, team members need an extra nudge to be innovative beyond their perceived limitations.

Recognize individuals and teamwork - I personally believe both are critical. Team recognition bolsters the team morale. Personal recognition provides a lot of individual motivation as well as urges others to rise to the challenge

Be ready to objectively explain individual recognition (or the lack of it) - As I mentioned above individual recognition is key in addition to collective recognition. However, remember that it is the *right* of other team members to challenge/question you on why they were not recognized. As a good manager, you should be able to give concrete responses as to why a team member was not recognized. If your responses are objective and non-confrontational, it will usually be accepted and taken as an input for self-improvement.

Before declaring a bad apple. - Remember that not everyone excels at every job. If you have assigned a person to be responsible in a particular area and that person is failing in his/her work, don't just decide the person is not "worthy" to be on your team. Often, a simple re-assignment to a different responsibility can change things drastically.

Be there in times of need. There will be a time for everyone when they face personal/family problems. Those who genuinely help during these times of need are those who form long lasting friendships. Do as much as possible to help your team get over hard times, should they seek your assistance. Remember this - jobs come and go, teams form and break but friendships last forever. When you genuinely help a person in time of need, this is never forgotten and loyalty builds.

Five Easy Steps for Motivation

How does management achieve motivation in the workplace in today's society? It is a great question, because a motivational workplace is a successful one. Without motivation the end result is poor quality in the workplace.

Some issues to consider when achieving motivation in the workplace are listed below. Every workplace has different situations. Not all rules will apply for unrelated settings. The corporate office will have different factors to consider than a factory, or a construction site. They are all going to be a little different. The one thing that will remain the same is human nature, and how we react to different situations.

Here are five common factors you can manage:

Different types of personalities

This is one of the biggest issues to consider. One thing that needs to be considered is that people are all different. We all have different personality traits and quirks. We are not always going to get along well every day, stuck in an office, kitchen, truck or factory together. It just isn't possible. It is not the way we are made. What one person may think of as constructive criticism, another may find as being bossy.

One person may think that they are being productive and the person next to them may think they are being lazy. It is just the way people think differently. Management's job is to see that the job is completed, through the employee. To do this, they must be able to understand the differences in people and learn how to deal with these issues. They need to learn to be diplomatic in these situations and keep everyone running smoothly.

Rewards

The key to motivation is reward for employees that mean something to them individually. So if motivation in the workplace is desired, then rewards for the employees are a must. They need to be motivated into doing a great job. Whether it is promotions, bonuses or just simple words of affirmation, they deserve that for a job well done.

Working environment

The workplace needs to be a fun and enjoyable place. A person spends 7-10 hours on the average per day at work. If it isn't a fun, and comfortable place to be, then workplace motivation can't be achieved.

Independency

Employees need to be able to think on their own. No one wants to be told what to do and when and how to do it every minute of the day. The employees need to know what the expectations are and be allowed to achieve them. They will take pride in their own idea and their own way of doing things. There is usually more than one way to accomplish the same thing.

Room for error

So many times, in the workplace, management does not plan for errors. Then when they happen, no one knows what to do to correct them. It is management's job to make a plan B just in case something goes wrong. And it does! To promote motivation in the workplace takes the manager time and patience. With these simple tips, it can be achieved and a more productive workplace can be found where people can work, socialize and laugh at the same time! It can be done

Making Effective Decisions

For performance of every single activity, decision making is unavoidable. Every small amount of work performed needs analysis of the options concerned. This is more so where the major activities are related to controlling and managing the work force. Decision-making is the tool of a manager that renders him, either effective or ineffective, depending upon his/her judgmental skills.

For a manager, it is necessary to understand that, a decision is a judgment or choice between two or more alternatives. It arises in an infinite number of situations, from the resolution of a problem to the implementation of a course of action. As managers handle a number of issues at the same time, the need to be aware and careful is more intense. Decision making is one activity that lies at the heart of management. A decision is a choice between a variety of alternatives, and a decision-maker is the one who makes the choice. Though decisions seem to be made quickly there is a long thought of future ramifications and guiding experience of the past, lead to that particular decision. Hence, Managers of people need to be adept decision-makers.

Identification

This is the phase of decision recognition. It includes such situations which generate opportunities, problems, and crises. Recognition of the need for a decision is triggered by information. That information forms a part of the ongoing flow of communications inside and outside the organization. At times, the decision-making originates just by a single stimulus, for example loss of an important customer. In other times the decision may be recognized after a long period of time, which has been triggered by a number of stimuli. Individuals receive information that indicates the need to make a decision, but that may not necessarily lead to decision–making activity. A decision maker is more likely to act if there appears to be a solution to the problem or the opportunity promises to help with a difficulty.

Development

The greatest amount of activity is concentrated in the developmental phase of the decision process. It leads to the development of one or more possible solutions to solve the problem or crisis. It also elaborates the choice of ways that are available for exploring an opportunity. This development phase is divided into two basic routines which are a search routine for locating ready-made solutions and a design routine to modify either found solutions or elaborate custom-made solutions.

Selection

Selection is not the single and final step in the decision process. It is a multistage process involving progressive deepening of the investigation of alternatives. A screening routine is appropriate to the extent that the search has provided more ready-made alternatives than can be intensively evaluated. At the end, the ready-made alternatives are either accepted or rejected.

Time

Decisions do not develop along a path of steady and undisturbed progress. Problems are encountered along the ways that have to be explored and, if possible, overcome. The decision takes place in the context of an organization that exists in a changing environment with new priorities emerging. The progress of a particular decision may need to be speeded up, slowed down or even delayed as new issues are presented to the organization and other decisions start to be developed. The whole process of decision-making is overshadowed by degree of uncertainty.

At the identification stage, there is the impact of individual's psychology, organizational perceptions and group-behavior. The past model the firm was built from affects this process. The existence of an opportunity, problem or crisis leads to recognition of the need for decision. The manager, in the development phase of the decision selects an alternative, either the one that has been tailor made or the one that is being followed for a long time. While selecting a particular course of decision, the goals, objectives and ethics need to be made the yard stick. The ultimate decision is adopted after the authorization from the top. Throughout the whole process there prevails an element of uncertainty, which the decision- maker tries to eliminate.

Types of Decision-Making

Irreversible

These types of decisions are those which, if made once cannot be unmade. Whatever is decided would then have its repercussions for a long time to come. It commits one irrevocably when there is no other satisfactory option to the chosen course. A manager should never use it as an all-or-nothing instant escape from general indecision.

Reversible

These types of decisions can be changed completely, before, during or after the agreed action begins. Such types of decisions allow one to acknowledge a mistake early in the process rather than perpetuate it. It can be effectively used for changing circumstances where reversal is necessary.

Experimental

These types of decisions are not final until the first results appear and prove themselves to be satisfactory. It requires positive feedback before one can decide on a course of action. It is useful and effective when the correct move is unclear but there is a clarity regarding general direction of action.

Trial and Error

In these types of decisions, knowledge is derived out of past mistakes. A certain course of action is selected and is tried out. If the results are positive, the action is carried further. If the results appear negative, another course is adopted. A trial is made and an error is occurred until the right combination is found. This allows the manager to adopt and adjust plans continuously before the full and final commitment. It uses both the positive and negative feedback before selecting one particular course of action.

Made in Stages

Here the decisions are made in steps until the whole action is completed. It allows close monitoring of risks as one accumulates the evidence of outcomes and obstacles at every stage. It permits feedback and further discussion before the next stage of the decision is made.

Cautious

It allows time for contingencies and problems that may crop up later at the time of implementation. The decision-makers hedge their best of efforts to adopt the right course. It helps to limit the risks that are inherent to decision- making. Although this may also limit the final gains. It allows one to scale down those projects which look too risky at first glance.

Conditional

Such types of decisions can be altered if certain foreseen circumstances arise. It is an either/or kind of decision with all options kept open. It prepares one to react if the competition makes a new move or if the game plan changes radically. It enables one to react quickly to the ever changing circumstances of competitive markets.

Delayed

Such decisions are put on hold till the decision–makers feel that the time is right. A go-ahead is given only when required elements are in place. It prevents one from making a decision at the wrong time or before all the facts are known. It may, at times result into forgoing of opportunities in the market that needs fast action.

Being Decisive

The ability to make timely, clear and firm decisions is an essential quality of leadership, but the type of decision needed varies according to the circumstances. Learning to recognize the implications of each type of decision leads to error minimization.

Being Positive

Taking decisive action does not mean making decisions on the spur of the moment. However, it may be necessary to make quick decisions in emergencies and also occasionally for other reasons. A true leader approaches the decisions confidently, being aware of what must be taken into account, and being fully in command of the decision–making process.

Making Fast Decisions

It is important to be able to assess whether a decision needs to be made quickly or whether it can wait. Good decision-makers often make instant decisions – but they must then assess the long-term implications.

Identyfying Issues

It is crucial to diagnose problems correctly. Before any decision is made identifying and defining the issue removes the criticality. This also means deciding who else needs to be involved in the issue, and analyzing what their involvement means.

Priortizing Factors

While making a decision, a manager needs to prioritize important factors. Some factors in a process are more important than others. The use of Pareto's rule of small few and trivial helps in setting up priorities. Giving every factor affecting a decision equal weight makes sense only if every factor is equally important; the Pareto rule concentrates on the significant 20 percent and gives the less important 80 percent lower priority.

Using Advisors

It is advisable to involve as many people as are needed in making a decision. In making collective decisions, specific expertise as well as experience of a person can be used simultaneously. The decision-maker, having weighed the advice of experts and experienced hands, must then use authority to ensure that the final decision is seen through.

Implementing a Decision

Decisions are valueless until they are translated into positive action, which in turn involves the decision maker in making a series of operational decisions and choices.

Making an Action Plan

A plan of action will begin to evolve naturally as options are narrowed and their feasibility is studied during the decision-making process. When developing a plan to implement a decision, everybody needs to fully understand the reason for that specific decision. An analysis of the overall task, determining what actions need to be taken and the manner in which the decision shall be implemented, should be provided in detail.

Delegating Action

Some decisions, which are simple, can be handled single handedly. But more complex decisions involve a number of tasks and the work of a team. Breaking each task into manageable chunks and delegating responsibility for planning to individuals within the team, makes the performance easier. The manager may delegate less complex matters to be decided by the subordinates, leaving more time for more important things.

Communicating a Decision

Once a decision is taken and planned, it needs to be relayed to the colleagues who are directly or indirectly affected by it. The release of information, if done properly, ensures that people understand exactly what has been decided and why, encouraging their support. Communicating the decision explanation of the course of action and why a particular course has been adopted, removes doubts and objections from the minds of the concerned parties.

Discussing the Progress of a Decision

Many meetings have no purpose but to discuss and inform. Meetings are specifically held to discuss progress in the implementation of a decision. Avoid wasting of time. While choosing a team for action the skills and personalities of the individuals should be taken into account.

Overcoming Objections

Decisions are likely to attract varying degrees of opposition, ranging from mild dissent to outright resistance. Rather than feeling aggrieved, opposition should be viewed as a valuable part of decision-making. Even if there is a need to push a decision through, simply ignoring objections or brushing them aside results into misunderstandings.

Remember

- Use your brightest people in decision-making.
- Work a demanding but realistic time-table.
- Before committing, rethink all the criteria involved.
- Never sacrifice the future for the short-term unless there is no option.
- A broad range of people, in the decision process brings in a lot of ideas.

Teambuilding

A team is a living, constantly changing and dynamic force in which a number of people come together to work. The members of the team discuss their objectives, assess ideas, make decisions and work towards their targets together. Teams out perform individuals acting alone, especially so when the performance requires multiple skills, judgments and experience.

All the successful teams are characterized by the same fundamental features:

- strong and effective leadership
- the establishment of precise objectives
- taking informed decisions, the ability to act quickly so as to carry forward these decisions
- communicating freely
- developing the necessary skills and techniques to fulfill the assigned tasks

The best way to understand teams is to look at their internal behavior. Their own stories reveal their accomplishments, skills, emotions, commitments and logical presentation. It is, however, the result of pursuing a demanding performance challenges.

The team is a basic unit of performance for most organizations. Successful team experiences are memorable because of what is accomplished and what each member learns in the process. Teams need to be flexible and responsive to changing events and demands, i.e. the demand of merging individual accountability with mutual accountability.

Hence, a team is a small number of people with complementary skills, who are committed to common purpose, performance goals and approach for which they hold themselves mutually accountable.

Successful teams can be formed by 2 to 22 or even more people, but more important than size is the shape, the pattern, and the spirit of the team is how the members divide up to perform their given tasks. The tasks that are to be performed by teams are basically categorized into three types.

- **Repetitive tasks:** require the members to assume a fixed role. These tasks are usually familiar work performance and can be fulfilled independently.
- **Projects:** require creative input from members though working in a fixed role. The major attribute is to work in unison and generate new products.
- **Partners:** demand constant and creative input and establishment of new work milestones. This style of working is more popular with senior levels of management.

Understanding Teams

- Teams are created when the performance demanded is challenging. The hunger for a challenge is the basic motivator.
- A disciplined outlook is necessary. Basics include size, purpose, goals, skills, approach and accountability for successful application.
- Organizations are divided into teams and sub–teams, the hierarchy of which ultimately leads to goal achievement.

- Teams at the top are the most difficult and complex in nature.
- There is a preference for group accountability over individual accountability by the people in the organization.
- Companies with strong performance standards seem to spawn more "real teams" than companies that promote teams per se.
- Hierarchy and teams go together almost as well as teams and performance.
- Integration of performance and learning are an inseparable part of team work.
- Organizational leaders can foster team performance best by building a strong performance ethic rather than by establishing a team – promoting environment alone.
- Biases do exist in teams.

Becoming the "Real Team"

The performance of a team depends upon the type of binding that exists between the group members. A working group relies primarily on the individual contributions of its members for group performance. A team striving for a magnified impact that is incremental to what its members could achieve in their individual roles forms gradually over a period of time resulting into cohesiveness.

Working groups

In such groups there are no significant incremental performance needs that would create the opportunity of turning this group into a productive and efficient team. In such groups, the members interact only to share information, discuss practices and to make decisions to help each individual perform effectively in his or her area of responsibility. It is just a small group that works together for getting the work done.

Pseudo-teams

In this type of group, though there exists a significant incremental performance of needs and opportunity, there is no focus on collective performance. There is no interest in a common purpose or set of performance goals, though they work in a group. Pseudo-teams are the weakest of all groups in terms of performance impact. Their contribution towards the company performance is less because the individual interest of each member detracts from each other. The sum of the whole is less than the potential of the individual parts.

Potential teams

In this type of group there is a considerable incremental performance need and the members really try to improve their performance impact. However, there is more for clarification of purpose, goals and working approach. It has not yet established collective accountability. Here the team approach starts making sense and performance impact becomes high. The most worthwhile performance gain comes in between the potential teams and real teams. Any movement pursued in this direction is worth trying.

Real teams

These are the teams with small number of people having complementary skills, which are equally committed to a common purpose, goals and work approach for which they hold themselves mutually accountable. Real teams are a basic unit of performance.

High – performance team

This group meets all the conditions of real teams and also has members deeply committed to one another's personal growth and success. This commitment is the soul of the group. They out - perform all other like teams. It is a powerful possibility and an excellent model for all "Real" and "Potential" teams.

Unlike teams, working groups rely on the sum of "individual bests" for their performance. Pseudo-teams do not take any risks and hence, remain where they are. Potential teams that take the risk to climb the curve and face obstacles and they turn into 'Real teams' and 'High performing teams'.

Building Team Performance

As such there is no guaranteed recipe for building team performance. Yet there are a variety of common approaches that can help potential teams take the necessary risk to grow in performance. To build up high performance, the following guidelines come in handy.

Establishing urgency and sense of direction

All team members need to believe that the team has urgent and worthwhile purposes. Performance expectations from team members should be clear. The members of the team need to realize that the task they are performing is important, that they will be a part of decisive accomplishment. The direction to be adopted for achievement should be clear.

The selection of the members should be on the basis of skills and not personality. Teams need complementary skills to perform the job. For effective performance, a mix of three different categories is helpful.

- Technical and functional skills.
- Problem solving skills
- Interpersonal skills

The right set of people is needed at the right place at the right time. Selection of team members is not only important for task forces and special project teams, but also ongoing groups. Too often there is a presumption that existing job status automatically warrants team membership. Hence, with selection, the job profile of the individual may be important, but most important is that the individual has the necessary skills for job performance.

More attention needs to be paid to first meetings and actions. Initial impression goes a long way. When the potential teams gather around for the first time, members alertly monitor the signals given by others to confirm, suspend or dispel known assumptions and concerns. First meetings usually are not the first time the team has ever met as a group. They are not necessarily limited to a single event. Too many potential teams fail to understand the importance of "first meetings" and instead allow existing habits and operating styles to dominate, including an overemphasis on individual instead of mutual accountability.

The rules regarding the clarity of behavior set a code of conduct. All real teams develop rules of conduct to help them achieve their purpose and performance goals. Rules are necessary for focus, openness, commitment and trust. The most critical rules may pertain to attendance, confidentiality, contributions, constructive confrontation and end-product orientation.

Few immediate performance-oriented tasks and goals bring team spirit. Most teams prepare immediate small tasks and performance oriented events that bring them together. Potential teams can set such events in motion by immediately establishing a few challenging, yet achievable, goals that can be reached early on. Significantly, the events generated by such stretch goals do not have to be successes. The focus is on achieving a spirit of being together.

Establishing fresh facts and information to keep the "challenge motivation". New information causes a potential team to redefine and enrich its understanding of the performance challenge, thereby helping the team reshape a common purpose, set clearer goals, and improve on its common approach. Potential teams with more permanent, ongoing assignments, on the other hand, easily develop habits that shut out new information and perspectives. New facts often bring such groups into renewed actions.

Spend time together. Teams must spend a lot of time together, especially at the beginning. Creative insights develop when personal bonding takes place. The more successful teams always find a way to spend extra time together.

Negotiating Skills

Negotiating is the process of communicating back and forth, for the purpose of reaching a joint agreement about differing needs or ideas. It is a collection of behaviors that involves communication, sales, marketing, psychology, sociology, assertiveness and conflict resolution. A negotiator may be a buyer or seller, a customer or supplier, a boss or employee, a business partner, a diplomat or a civil servant.

On a more personal level, negotiation takes place between spouse's friends, parents or children. It is a process of interaction between two or more parties jointly involved in an outcome, who initially have different objectives. They use argument and persuasion to resolve their difference in order to achieve a mutually acceptable solution. Another important consideration is that negotiation implies acceptance by both parties that agreement between them is required before a decision can be implemented.

The art of negotiation is based on attempting to reconcile what constitutes a good result for the other party. To achieve a situation where both sides win something for themselves, you need to be well prepared, alert and flexible. There are seven basic principles common to all forms of negotiation.

- There is a minimum of two parties involved in the negotiation process. There exists some common interest, either in the subject matter of the negotiation or in the negotiating context that puts or keeps the parties in contact.
- Though the parties have the same degree of interest, they initially start with different opinions and objectives which hinder the outcome in general.
- In the beginning, parties consider that negotiation is a better way of trying to solve their differences.
- Each party is under an impression that there is a possibility of persuading the other party to modify their original position. Initially parties feel that they shall maintain their opening position and persuade the other to change.
- During the process, the ideal outcome proves unattainable but parties retain their hope of an acceptable final agreement.
- Each party has some influence or power – real or assumed – over the other's ability to act.
- The process of negotiation is that of interaction between people – usually this is direct and verbal interchange.

Negotiation is a skill that anyone can learn and practice. The necessary skills required for successful negotiations can be listed as:

- The ability to define a range of objectives yet be flexible about some of them.
- The ability to explore the possibilities of a wide range of options.
- The ability to be well prepared.
- The ability to listen to and question other parties.
- The ability to set priorities.

These are useful abilities, not only in negotiations but in daily life as well. It is useful to remember that the ability to influence and persuade is one of the most essential of all management skills – and influence and persuasion are very much the stuff of effective negotiation.

Types of Negotiation in Organizations

Depending upon the situation and time, the way the negotiations are to be conducted differs. The skills of negotiations depend and differ widely from one situation to the other. Basically negotiation types can be divided into three broad categories.

Day-to-day / Managerial Negotiations

Such types of negotiations are done within the organization and are related to the internal problems in the organization. It is in regards to the working relationship between the groups of employees. Usually, the manager needs to interact with the members at different levels in the organization structure. For conducting the day-to-day business, internally, the superior needs to allot job responsibilities, maintain a flow of information, direct the record keeping and many more activities for smooth functioning. All this requires entering into negotiations with the parties internal to the organization.

Commercial Negotiations

Such types of negotiations are conducted with external parties. The driving forces behind such negotiations are usually financial gains. They are based on a give-and-take relationship. Commercial negotiations successfully end up into contracts. It relates to foregoing of one resource to get the other.

Legal Negotiations

These negotiations are usually formal and legally binding. Disputes over precedents can become as significant as the main issue. They are also contractual in nature and relate to gaining legal ground.

Is Negotiation Necessary?

Negotiation, at times, can be a lengthy and cumbersome process. By asking whether it is necessary, time may sometimes be saved and unnecessary compromise avoided. On occasions, a request to negotiate may best be met by pointing out that the party making the request has no standing in the matter. If a manager has the undoubted authority to act, making a decision rather than negotiating about it may be the best tactic.

Alternatively, there are cases in which the best response to a request or a claim is to concede it without argument. Why waste time negotiating if the other party has a good case and there are no adverse consequences in conceding? Unnecessary negotiation, followed, perhaps, by a grudging concession of the other party's claim, will lose all the advantage that might be gained with a quick unexpected yes.

An alternative to a simple yes or no when a difference of view occurs is to skip negotiation and proceed immediately to some form of third – party intervention. On the most formal basis, this might imply a decision to take a dispute to court. On an informal basis two managers who quickly realize that they cannot reach agreement about a working problem may jointly agree to stop wasting time in argument and refer the matter to a senior manager for resolution.

It is good to follow this general rule: Do not negotiate unless you have to – or unless you can obtain some direct or indirect advantage by doing so.

Process of Negotiation

The whole process of negotiation can be broadly divided into 3 stages:

- A preparation phase before the negotiation begins.
- The actual process of negotiating.
- The implementation and follow up of the agreement.

The preparation for a successful negotiation process is essential. The achievement of the target has to be a systematic and strategic move. It is necessary to obtain a detailed and minute analysis. A manager needs to be clear about his perspective.

Evaluate relative strengths

Before embarking on negotiation, there is a need to assess the party's relative strengths. This strength can be defined as the power to influence others so as to have an upper hand over the final outcome. Each side has certain bargaining powers on the back of which the whole negotiating process can be carried. While weighing relative strengths, the judgment regarding four things is involved:

- The amount of authority that each party possesses to conduct negotiations and the ability of the parties to make decisions.
- The strength of each party to get sanctions or benefits that is unrelated to the matter under negotiation.
- The logic or equity in the arguments.
- The firm determination with which each party pursues its case.

Set the objectives

While planning negotiations, an assessment of relative strengths should be linked to the determination of objectives. Usually, the stronger one's position is, the higher the level of objective achievement. The passing of the agreement takes place depending upon three different possible settlement levels.

- The ideal or the best possible deal.
- The expected settlement level.

- The worst, though still just acceptable deal.

As a negotiator, one needs to identify the top line objectives, the best achievable outcome and the outcome that can be acceptable at the lowest level. It is vital to consider the other party's viewpoint as well as one's own. One objective of negotiations is to help the other party feel satisfied with the outcome and not to be too aggressive in the process.

Keep an eye on the other side

For conducting successful negotiation, an eye on the other party's plans, strengths and weaknesses helps in deciding a winning strategy. What are the objectives of the other party? What are the facts and arguments they are likely to put forward and their overall winning strategy? All this knowledge is useful for being prepared about the underlying and unstated issues. Besides, exchanging factual data before negotiations helps in overcoming delays or confusions. Checking of the issue, detailing facts and arguments, exchanging details are all preparatory assessments.

Decision regarding the style and the scene

This is planning of the more actual negotiation. Negotiations can be conducted in a number of different styles. They can be discursive or brisk, formal or informal, assertive or persuasive. Depending upon the role and responsibility of the individual their styles differ. Whom to involve in the discussion process and whom not to involve, is a crucial task. Minutest details like the location of the negotiation site, the seating arrangements, refreshments to be provided, and documentation aspects all need special attention. Negotiations are surely affected by the style, pace and composition of the negotiating teams but equally important are the seating plans, breaks and conducting of the session itself. It is also useful to keep some record of the outcome of negotiations to ensure a common understanding.

Setting of the Agenda

It is important to chalk out a plan of action in advance to avoid misunderstandings and common errors. If a clear cut guideline regarding what is to be done is provided, a lot of time and effort can be saved. The agenda may be formal or informal. If the subject, scope and purpose are fixed in advance, confusion can be avoided. It is useful to remember that the progress of negotiation is influenced significantly by the first speaker. One way of securing a strong opening position is to volunteer a brief rehearsal of the background before full negotiations begin.

Pleading your case

To win the maximum favor in negotiation, tactics have to be used to strengthen one's position during the bargaining process. Prior to introducing a new issue, its acceptability by the opposite parties needs to be rated. Compromise and concession are the essential aspects of negotiation. Equally necessary is the attachment of conditions to the concessions.

The use of emotion in negotiating should be avoided. At times during discussions, people start getting emotionally attached. It is professionally dangerous to rise to the bait of personal attack. There are two occasions, when a controlled display of emotion may be beneficial. The emotion must be sincere and its use should be a conscious decision, not an instant reaction.

It is advantageous for a good negotiator to be a good listener. The most common fault occurs in saying too much and listening too little. To keep the heaviness out, use of humor reduces the tension. Use of humor also avoids a confrontational mode.

Experienced negotiators usually do not commit themselves to definite statements until they are confident that this will not prejudice their position. The art of reading between the lines helps in avoiding perceptional errors.

Timing and Adjournments

The maximum time for which an individual can maintain continuous attention and involvement, is somewhere around two hours. Henceforth, while planning negotiations, thought needs to be given to the time-scale.

The most ideal time allotment for presentations is 15 to 20 minutes and the ideal time for individual contribution is two to three minutes at the beginning of the discussion.

Breaks and adjournments are a helpful reprieve from monotonous discussions. They provide time to consider progress or new proposals within the team and avoid rash decisions. It also helps in bringing an end to unconstructive and personalized arguments. Besides, during the adjournment sessions the parties can have an opportunity for informal and casual talks.

Arriving at an agreement

The closer the negotiation comes to end, the more careful the discussion needs to be handled. While weighing the benefits of the agreement, besides immediate returns, the quality of long–term relationships should be the crux. The final offer and agreement needs to be timed to coincide with the positive and constructive discussion. Before finalizing, it is advisable to check that all aspects in the deal have been taken care of, particularly dates for implementation, completion time and definition and meaning of each term. Ensure that both parties fully understand what has been agreed and get the confirmation in writing. Those issues that still remain unsolved can be carried forward for future negotiations.

Effective Implementation

Arriving at an agreement is not an end in itself. The purpose with which negotiations are carried is to reach an outcome or action. An agreement is not successful until it has been effectively implemented. Adequate information and explanation should be supplied to those who are affected.

Handling Breakdown

It is not necessary that negotiations always prove successful. At times an agreement may not be achieved and this requires other arrangements. A contingency plan should be kept ready in case of failure of the negotiations. The major options for handling breakdowns are either to go ahead on your own and take a decision that is best or seek third party intervention.

Handling Difficult Negotiators

Every person that the manager negotiates with may not necessarily be easy to deal with. Some negotiators turn aggressive to create an impression of their being tough. Instead of getting intimidated, winning is more important. To handle such outrageous behavior:

- Speak more quietly than them.
- Have more space in between your words than them.
- If they interrupt, pause for a few seconds after they finish.
- Be critical of foul language.
- Do not rise to bait if they attack or blame you.
- Ignore all threats.

Tactics

Making Threats - Certain threatful conditions need to be put in the negotiation deal. A warning of unwelcome repercussions, if one fails to agree to the terms of offer need to be emphasized. A fear of penalties avoids waste of effort and resources.

- **Counter Tactics** - It is advisable to state to the other party that negotiations are not possible under stress. A review of the other options available can be made only on the basis of the merit of the case.

Offering Tactics - Questions regarding the performance of the Company and professional competence of negotiators amount to insults. Another way of adding insults is to criticize the quality of the product or service.

- **Counter Tactics** - Stay calm. Do not lose your temper or offer insults in return. State your position firmly and lead the conversation towards constructive negotiations.

Bluffing - In bluffing, punitive action without being too specific are given. People, at times also make dubious assertions.

- **Counter Tactics** - Call off such bluffs. Refuse to agree to the other party's terms and wait for a reaction. Question all statements, and ask for evidence to support any claims that appear dubious.

Using Intimidation - Keeping one waiting, making one sit in an uncomfortable or awkward place and receiving phone call or visitors during negotiations are all signs of Intimidation

- **Counter Tactics** - These are plays to make one feel less confident. Recognize it. The original terms should not be dropped unless concessions have been gained.

Divide and Rule -It is trying to develop a line between the members of the opposite team by exploiting potential disagreements among them and appealing to the person most sympathetic to the case.

- **Counter Tactics** - It is advisable to brief team members in advance and decide on a position that is acceptable to everyone. The meeting should be adjourned if a difference of opinion arises within the team members.

Using Leading Questions - Asking such questions leads to declare a weakness in the negotiating position which ultimately forces concessions.

- **Counter Tactics** - It is better to avoid answering questions, where the intention and meaning is unclear. It is advisable to attach concessions to such conditions.

Making Emotional Appeals - This is done through accusing one of acting unfairly and not agreeing to the terms and conditions. At times there is also an offense created by lack of trust.

- **Counter Tactics** - Be fair on the commitment of achieving a fair settlement on business terms. Questions should be asked to test the validity of manipulative claims. Lead the conversation back to discussing the issues.

Testing the Boundaries - Gaining on additional concessions through minor infringements of the terms agreed, resulting in substantial gain over a long period.

- **Counter Tactics** - One should be clear on exactly what the agreement is about. Draw up a clearly worded statement of the terms agreed and hold the other party to these at all times.

CHAPTER 3
HOW TO WRITE A BUSINESS PLAN

Business Plan Overview

The Executive Summary: While appearing first, this section of the business plan is written last. It summarizes the key elements of the entire business plan.

The Industry: This is an overview of the industry sector that your business will be a part of, including industry trends, major players in the industry, and estimated industry sales. This section of the business plan will also include a summary of your business's place within the industry.

Market Analysis: This is an examination of the primary target market for your product or service, including geographic location, demographics, your target market's needs and how these needs are being met currently.

Competitive Analysis: This is an investigation of your direct and indirect competitors, with an assessment of their competitive advantage and an analysis of how you will overcome any entry barriers to your chosen market.

Marketing Plan: This is a detailed explanation of your sales strategy, pricing plan, proposed advertising and promotion activities, and product or service's benefits.

Management Plan: This is an outline of your business's legal structure and management resources, including your internal management team, external management resources, and human resources needs.

Operating Plan: This is a description of your business's physical location, facilities and equipment, kinds of employees needed, inventory requirements and suppliers, and any other applicable operating details, such as a description of the manufacturing process.

Financial Plan: This is a description of your funding requirements, your detailed financial statements, and a financial statement analysis.

Appendices and Exhibits: This includes any additional information that will help establish the credibility of your business idea, such as marketing studies, photographs of your product, and/or contracts or other legal agreements pertinent to your business.

Writing the Executive Summary

The purpose of the executive summary of the business plan is to provide your readers with an overview of the business plan. Think of it as an introduction to your business. Therefore, your business plan's executive summary will include summaries of:

- a description of your company, including your products and/or services
- your mission statement
- your business's management
- the market and your customer
- marketing and sales
- your competition
- your business's operations
- financial projections and plans

The executive summary will end with a summary statement, a "last kick at the can" sentence or two designed to persuade the readers of your business plan that your business is a winner.

To write the executive summary of the business plan, start by following the list above and writing one to three sentences about each topic. If you have trouble crafting these summary sentences from scratch, review your business plan to get you going. In fact, one approach to writing the executive summary of the business plan is to take a summary sentence or two from each of the business plan sections you've already written. Then finish your business plan's executive summary with a clinching closing sentence or two that answers the reader's question "Why is this winning business?"

For example, a business plan's executive summary for a pet-sitting business might conclude: "The loving on-site professional care that Pet Grandma will provide is sure to appeal to both cat and dog owners throughout the St. Louis area."

Tips for Writing the Business Plan's Executive Summary

- Focus on providing a summary. The business plan itself will provide the details and whether bank managers or investors, the readers of your business plan don't want to have their time wasted.
- Keep your language strong and positive. Don't weaken the executive summary of your business plan with weak language. Instead of writing, "Dogstar Industries might be in an excellent position to win government contracts", write "Dogstar Industries will be in an excellent position..."
- The executive summary should be no more than two pages long. Resist the temptation to pad your business plan's executive summary with details (or pleas). The job of the executive summary is to present the facts and entice your reader to read the rest of the business plan, not tell him everything.
- Polish your executive summary. Read it aloud. Does it flow or does it sound choppy? Is it clear and succinct? Once it sounds good to you, have someone else who knows nothing about your business read it and make suggestions for improvement.
- Tailor the executive summary of your business plan to your audience. If the purpose of your business plan is to entice investors, for example, your executive summary should focus

on the opportunity your business provides investors and why the opportunity is special.

- Put yourself in your readers' place... and read your executive summary again. Does this executive summary generate interest or excitement in the reader? If not, why?

Remember, the executive summary of your business plan will be the first thing that is read. If it is poorly written, it will also be the last!

The Industry Section

When writing your business plan, the Industry section is best organized into two parts: an overview of the industry and a summary of your business' position within the industry. Before writing this section of the business plan, use these questions to focus your research:

- What is the size of your industry?
- What sectors does this industry include?
- Who are the major players in this industry?
- What are the markets and customers for this industry?
- What are the industry's estimated sales this year? Last year? The year before?
- What national/economic trends have affected this industry and how?
- What national/economic trends might affect it in the future and how?
- What is the long-term outlook for this industry?
- What products or services will your business be selling?
- What is your Unique Selling Proposition? (What is it about your business that makes it unique and sets it apart from competitors?)
- What are the barriers to entry in your industry?
- How will you overcome these barriers?
- Who are your competitors?

- What is the market share of your competitors?
- What is your business' competitive advantage (i.e. your market niche or estimated market share)?

What is your target market?

How are you protecting your product or process (i.e. patents, copyrights, and trademarks, franchise rights that you either hold or plan to acquire)?

Once you have all this information, you'll write this section of the business plan in the form of several short paragraphs. (Remember, each of these paragraphs is a summary, not a detailed point-by-point explanation.)

Conducting Business Plan Research for the Industry Overview

When you're researching a business plan and looking for information on industries, the web sites will give you information and statistics. The business sections of national newspapers and business magazines will also be helpful; these often carry features on past and future business trends.

The Market Analysis Section

When writing a business plan, the focus of the Market Analysis section is a thorough examination of your target market, those people that you intend to sell your products or services to. The first step is to define your target market. Even if you intend on selling a service only in your own town, you're not selling that service to everyone who lives there. You need to know exactly what the people who might be interested in buying your product or service are like, and how many of them there are. Then you need to make some projections about them, in terms of how much of your products or service they might buy, and how they might be affected by trends and policies.

As always when you're writing a business plan, research is the key. Before writing the Market Analysis section of the business plan, use these general questions to start your research about your targeted markets:

- How old are they?
- What gender are they?
- Where do they live?
- What is their family structure (number of children, extended family, etc.)?
- What is their income?
- What do they do for a living?
- What is their lifestyle like?
- How do they like to spend their spare time?
- What motivates them?
- What is the size of your target market?

Further to define your target market, you need to ask the specific questions that are directly related to your products or services. For instance, if you plan to sell computer-related services, you need to know things such as how many computers your prospective customer owns. If you plan on selling garden furniture and accessories, you need to know what kinds of garden furniture or accessories your potential customers have bought in the past, and how often.

Projections about the Target Market

- What proportion of your target market has used a product similar to yours before?
- How much of your product or service might your target market buy? (Estimate this in gross sales and/or in units of product/service sold.)
- What proportion of your target market might be repeat customers?
- How might your target market be affected by demographic shifts?
- How might your target market be affected by economic events (e.g. a local mill closing or a big-box retailer opening locally)?

- How might your target market be affected by larger socioeconomic trends?
- How might your target market be affected by government policies (e.g. new bylaws or changes in taxes)?

The Market Analysis Section

Once you have all this information, you'll write the Market Analysis in the form of several short paragraphs. Use appropriate headings for each paragraph. If you have several target markets, you may want to number each. Remember to properly cite your sources of information within the body of your Market Analysis as you write it. You and other readers of your business plan will need to know the sources of the statistics or opinions that you've gathered from others.

Research

The local library, the local Chamber of Commerce, Board of Trade, City Hall, Economic Development Centre, local government agent's office, local phone book and yellow pages will all have information that will help you define your target market and provide insights into trends. These are all secondary sources of information. You may also want to conduct your own market research (use primary data). For instance, you might want to design a questionnaire and survey your target market to learn more about their habits and preferences relating to your product or service.

Does all this sound time-consuming? It is!

But it needs to be done if your business plan is going to have any validity. You can have the most fantastic product or service in the world, but if no one's interested in buying it, it will just gather dust. If you don't have the time or the research skills to thoroughly define your target market yourself, hiring a person or firm to do the market research for you can be a wise investment.

The Competitive Analysis Section

The competitive analysis section can be the most difficult section to compile when writing a business plan. Before you can analyze your competitors, you have to investigate them. The first step of preparing your competitive analysis is to determine who your competitors are. This isn't the hard part. If you're planning to start a small business that's going to operate locally, you can identify your competitors just by driving around or looking in the local phone book. The main question for you will be one of range; if your business plan is centered on the idea of opening a bakery, how far will customers be willing to drive to get fresh buns or bread?

However, it may be that your local business will also had non-local competitors. If I'm selling office supplies, for instance, I may also have to compete with big-box retailers within a driving distance of several hours, mail order companies, and companies that offer office supplies online. You want to make sure that you identify all your possible competitors at this stage.

Secondly, you need to gather the information about your competition that you need for the competitive analysis. This can be the difficult. While you can always approach your competitors directly, they may or may not be willing to tell you what you need to know to put together this section of your business plan.

You need to know:

- What markets or market segments your competitors serve
- What benefits your competition offers
- Why customers buy from them
- As much as possible about their products and/or services, pricing, and promotion.

Gathering Information on Competitors

A visit is still the most obvious starting point - either to the bricks and mortar store, or to the company's web site. You can learn a lot about your competitor's products and services, pricing, and even promotion strategies by visiting their business site, and may even be able to deduce quite a bit about the benefits your competitor offers. Go there and look around thoroughly.

Watch how customers are treated. Check out the prices. You can also learn a fair bit about your competitors from talking to their customers and/or clients - if you know who they are. With a bricks and mortar local competitor, you might be able to find out about the reasons customers buy from them by canvassing friends and acquaintances locally. Other good "live" sources of information about competitors include a company's vendors or suppliers, and a company's employees. They may or may not be willing to talk to you, but it's worth seeking them out and asking.

Watch for trade shows that your competitors may be attending. Businesses are there to disseminate information about and sell their products or services. Attending and visiting their booths may be an excellent way to find out about your competitors. You'll also want to search for the publicly available information about your competitors. Newspapers, magazines, and online publications may all have information about the company you're investigating for your competitive analysis. Press releases may be particularly useful.

Once you've compiled the information about your competitors, you're ready to analyze it.

Analyzing the Competition

The competitive analysis section of the business plan is not just a list of information about your competitors. It's the analysis of the information that's important. Study the information you've gathered about each of your competitors and ask yourself this primary question: **How are you going to compete with that company?**

For many small businesses, the key to competing successfully is to identify a market niche where they can capture a specific target market whose needs are not being met. Is there a particular segment of the market that your competition has overlooked? For example, if you hope to start a book store, and your competitor sells all kinds of books to all kinds of people, might you be able to specialize in children's books, or educational books and supplies?

Remember; you don't have to go into exhaustive detail here, but you do need to persuade the reader of your business plan that you are knowledgeable about the competition and that you have a clear, definitive plan that will enable your new business to successfully compete.

The Marketing Plan Section

The Marketing Plan section explains how you're going to get your customers to buy your products and/or services. The marketing plan, then, will include sections detailing your:

- Products and/or Services and your Unique Selling Proposition
- Pricing Strategy
- Sales/Distribution Plan
- Advertising and Promotions Plan

The easiest way to develop your marketing plan is to work through each of these sections, referring to the market research you completed when you were writing the previous sections of the business plan.

(Note that if you are developing a marketing plan on its own, rather than as part of a business plan, the marketing plan will also need to include a Target Market and a Competitive Analysis section.

Products and/or Services

This part of the marketing plan focuses on the uniqueness of your product or service, and how the customer will benefit from using the products or services you're offering. Use these questions to write a paragraph summarizing these aspects for your marketing plan:

What are the features of your product or service?

Describe the physical attributes of your product or service, and any other relevant features, such as what it does, or how your product or service differs from competitive products or services.

How will your product or service benefit the customer?

Remember that benefits can be intangible as well as tangible; for instance, if you're selling a cleaning product, your customers will benefit by having a cleaner house, but they may also benefit by enjoying better health. Brainstorm as many benefits as possible to begin with, and then choose to emphasize the benefits that your targeted customers will most appreciate in your marketing plan. What is it that sets your product or service apart from all the rest? In other words, what is your Unique Selling Proposition, the message you want your customers to receive about your product or service that is the heart of your marketing plan? The marketing plan is all about communicating this central message to your customers.

Pricing Strategy

The pricing strategy portion of the marketing plan involves determining how you will price your product or service; the price you charge has to be competitive but still allow you to make a reasonable profit. The keyword here is "reasonable.

You can charge any price you want to, but for every product or service there's a limit to how much the consumer is willing to pay. Your pricing strategy needs to take this consumer threshold into account.

The most common question small business people have about the pricing strategy section of the marketing plan is, "How do you know what price to charge?" Basically you set your pricing through a process of calculating your costs, estimating the benefits to consumers, and comparing your products, services, and prices to others that are similar.

Set your pricing by examining how much it costs you to produce the product or service and adding a fair price for the benefits that the customer will enjoy. Examining what others are charging for similar products or services will guide you when you're figuring out what a "fair" price for such benefits would be. You may find it useful to conduct a Breakeven Analysis.

The pricing strategy you outline in your marketing plan will answer the following questions:

What is the cost of your product or service? Make sure you include all your fixed and variable costs when you're calculating this. The cost of labor and materials are obvious, but you may also need to include freight costs, administrative costs, and/or selling costs, for example.

How does the pricing of your product or service compare to the market price of similar products or services?

Explain how the pricing of your product or service is competitive. For instance, if the price you plan to charge is lower, why are you able to do this? If it's higher, why would your customer be willing to pay more? This is where the "strategy" part of the pricing strategy comes into play. Will your business be more competitive if you charge more, less, or the same as your competitors and why?

What kind of ROI (Return on Investment) are you expecting with this pricing strategy, and within what time frame?

Sales Plan

Remember, the primary goal of the marketing plan is to get people to buy your products or services. The Sales and Distribution part of the marketing plan details how this is going to happen.

Advertising And Promotion Plan

Essentially the Advertising and Promotion section of the marketing plan describes how you're going to deliver your Unique Selling Proposition to your prospective customers.

Advertising - The best approach to advertising is to think of it in terms of media and which media will be most effective in reaching your target market. Then you can make decisions about how much of your annual advertising budget you're going to spend on each medium. What percentage of your annual advertising budget will you invest in each of the following:

- the internet
- television
- radio
- newspapers
- magazines
- telephone books/directories
- billboards
- bench/bus/subway ads
- direct mail
- Cooperative advertising with wholesalers, retailers or other businesses?

Include not only the cost of the advertising but your projections about how much business the advertising will bring in.

Sales Promotion - If it's appropriate to your business, you may want to incorporate sales promotion activities into your advertising and promotion plan, such as:

- offering free samples
- coupons
- point of purchase displays
- product demonstrations

Marketing Materials - Every business will include some of these in their promotion plans. The most common marketing material is the business card, but brochures, pamphlets and service sheets are also common.

Publicity - Another avenue of promotion that every business should use. Describe how you plan to generate publicity. While press releases are common, that's only one way to get people spreading the word about your business. You need to consider:

- product launches

- special events, including community involvement
- writing articles
- getting and using testimonials

Your Business' Web Site - If your business has or will have a web site, describe how your web site fits into your advertising and promotion plan.

Tradeshows - Tradeshows can be incredibly effective promotions and sales opportunities - if you pick the right ones and go equipped to put your promotion plan into action.

Remember no business is too small to have a marketing plan.

The Management Plan Section

The Management Plan section describes your management team and staff and how your business ownership is structured. People reading your business plan will be looking to see not only who's on your management team but how the skills of your management and staff will contribute to the bottom line.

The basic business categories of Sales and Marketing, Administration and Production work for many small businesses. You may find that your company needs additional management categories such as Research and Development and/or Human Resources. It's not necessary to have a different person in charge of each business management category , some key management people may fill more than one role. Identify the key management people in your business and explain what functions each team member will fill.

This is your management team outline. You may wish to present this as an organizational chart in your business plan, although list format is fine.

Along with this outline, the management plan will include complete resumes of each member of your management team, and an explanation of how each person's skills will contribute to your business' success.

Your External Management Team

Besides your internal management team, those reading your business plan will be extremely interested in knowing how you plan to use external management resources. Think of external management resources as your internal management team's backup. There are two main sources of external management resources you should utilize and describe in this section of the business plan; Professional Services and an Advisory Board. It's a smart move to set up an Advisory Board for your business as soon as possible.

An Advisory Board is like a management think tank; the members of your Advisory Board will provide you with additional advice to run your business profitably and well. If you choose your board members carefully, they can also provide expertise that your internal management team lacks.

The Operating Plan Section

When writing the business plan, the operating plan section describes the physical necessities of your business' operation, such as your business' physical location, facilities and equipment. Depending on what kind of business you'll be operating, it may also include information about inventory requirements and suppliers, and a description of the manufacturing process.

Keeping focused on the bottom line will help you organize this part of the business plan; think of the operating plan as an outline of the capital and expense requirements your business will need to operate from day to day. You need to do two things for your readers in the operating section of the business plan: show what you've done so far to get your business off the ground and demonstrate that you understand the manufacturing or delivery process of producing your product or service.

The Financial Plan Section

The financial plan section is the section that determines whether or not your business idea is viable, and is a key component in determining whether or not your business plan is going to be able to attract any investment in your business idea. Basically, the financial plan section of the business plan consists of three financial statements, the income statement, the cash flow projection and the balance sheet and a brief explanation/analysis of these three statements.

Think of your business expenses as broken into two categories; your start up expenses and your operating expenses. All the costs of getting your business up and running go into the start up expenses category. These expenses may include:

- business registration fees
- business licensing and permits
- starting inventory
- rent deposits
- down payments on property
- down payments on equipment
- utility set up fees

Operating expenses are the costs of keeping your business running. Think of these as the things you're going to have to pay each month. Your list of operating expenses may include:

- salaries (yours and staff salaries)
- rent or mortgage payments
- telecommunications
- utilities
- raw materials
- storage
- distribution
- promotion
- loan payments
- office supplies
- maintenance

Once again, this is just a partial list to get you going. Once you have your operating expenses list complete, the total will show you what it will cost you to keep your business running each month. Multiply this number by 6, and you have a six month estimate of your operating expenses. Then add this to the total of your start up expenses list, and you'll have a ballpark figure for your complete start up costs.

The Income Statement

The Income Statement is one of the three financial statements that you need to include in the Financial Plan section of the business plan. The Income Statement shows your Revenues, Expenses, and Profit for a particular period. It's a snapshot of your business that shows whether or not your business is profitable at that point in time; Revenue - Expenses = Profit/Loss.

While established businesses normally produce an Income Statement each fiscal quarter, or even once each fiscal year, for the purposes of the business plan, an Income Statement should be generated more frequently - monthly for the first year.

The Cash Flow Projection

The Cash Flow Projection shows how cash is expected to flow in and out of your business. For you, it's an important tool for cash flow management, letting you know when your expenditures are too high or when you might want to arrange short term investments to deal with a cash flow surplus. As part of your business plan, a Cash Flow Projection will give you a much better idea of how much capital investment your business idea needs.

For a bank loans officer, the Cash Flow Projection offers evidence that your business is a good credit risk and that there will be enough cash on hand to make your business a good candidate for a line of credit or short term loan.

Do not confuse a Cash Flow Projection with a Cash Flow Statement. The Cash Flow Statement shows how cash has flowed in and out of your business. In other words, it describes the cash flow that has occurred in the past. The Cash Flow Projection shows the cash that is anticipated to be generated or expended over a chosen period of time in the future.

While both types of Cash Flow reports are important business decision-making tools for businesses, we're only concerned with the Cash Flow Projection in the business plan. You will want to show Cash Flow Projections for each month over a one year period as part of the Financial Plan portion of your business plan.

There are three parts to the Cash Flow Projection.

The first part details your Cash Revenues. Enter your estimated sales figures for each month. Remember that these are Cash Revenues; you will only enter the sales that are collectible in cash during the specific month you are dealing with.

The second part is your Cash Disbursements. Take the various expense categories from your ledger and list the cash expenditures you actually expect to pay that month for each month.

The third part of the Cash Flow Projection is the Reconciliation of Cash Revenues to Cash Disbursements. As the word "reconciliation" suggests, this section starts with an opening balance which is the carryover from the previous month's operations. The current month's Revenues are added to this balance; the current month's Disbursements are subtracted, and the adjusted cash flow balance is carried over to the next month.

Remember, the Closing Cash Balance is carried over to the next month. Once again, to use this template for your own business, you will need to delete and add the appropriate Revenue and Disbursement categories that apply to your own business.

The main danger when putting together a Cash Flow Projection is being over optimistic about your projected sales. Once you have your Cash Flow Projections completed, it's time to move on to the Balance Sheet.

The Balance Sheet

The Balance Sheet is the last of the financial statements that you need to include in the Financial Plan section of the business plan. The Balance Sheet presents a picture of your business' net worth at a particular point in time. It summarizes all the financial data about your business, breaking that data into 3 categories; assets, liabilities, and equity. Some definitions first:

Assets are tangible objects of financial value that are owned by the company.

A liability is a debt owed to a creditor of the company.

Equity is the net difference when the total liabilities are subtracted from the total assets.

All accounts in your General Ledger are categorized as an asset, a liability or equity.

The relationship between them is expressed in this equation: Assets = Liabilities + Equity.

For the purposes of your business plan, you'll be creating a pro forma Balance Sheet intended to summarize the information in the Income Statement and Cash Flow Projections. Normally a business prepares a Balance Sheet once a year.

Once you have your Balance Sheet completed, you're ready to write a brief analysis of each of the three financial statements. When you're writing these analysis paragraphs, you want to keep them short and cover the highlights, rather than writing an in-depth analysis.

CHAPTER 4
SUCCESSFUL TRADE SHOWS

How To Pick A Trade Show

With more than 9,000 Trade Shows and public expositions being held each year, choosing the right one can be a daunting task. The difficulty of making these choices is one of the reasons why some companies do not exhibit at all. Making the wrong choice can be a costly mistake. Yet there are many resources available that can provide the information we need to choose the shows that will be most productive for our company, and yield the greatest return on our exhibit investment.

The following are other key factors about trade shows that should be noted:

- The average sales call costs $229.70.
- To close an order, 5.5 sales calls on average are required, bringing the cost to $1,263.35.
- The cost per contact at a Trade Show is approximately $106.70 with an average of 0.8 follow-up calls required to close the sale. That results in a savings of $1,053.89 per order.
- Contacting your entire current prospective base for the most part is an impossible task, supported by the following statistic: 92% of attendees at regional shows and 84% of attendees at national shows have not been contacted by the exhibiting business during the prior year.
- 83% of show attendees, visiting an exhibit, had not seen a salesperson from that company during the previous 12 months.

- 78% of 1st time show attendees and 85% of the veterans have buying authority.
- 61% plan to buy something exhibited at a show.
- 54% of show inquiries do not require a follow up call.
- It costs 70% less to close a trade show lead than a field sales call,
- 45% of all sales leads from a show will turn into a sale for someone within a year.
- 75-90% of the inquiries, at a show, are never followed up.

To determine if you should exhibit in a particular trade show or public show, you have to answer the following two questions:

- Will the people you want to reach be there?
- Will the show management be an effective matchmaker?

The following are the key questions and measurement criteria that you will need to have established as a benchmark for determining the trade show participation reflected within this plan:

Who have attended the show in the past? Show brochures generally trumpet the number of attendees at the previous show, but what does the number represent? It is far more important to know who is attending, than how many.

Ask for the attendee profile. The demographic data a show manager provides can help us to evaluate both the audience and the show manager's research. We will need to see last year's registration form. Comprehensive data are gathered by computerized registration systems used at many trade shows today. They record each attendee's company name, size, and location; the individual's job title, buying authority, purchase intentions, budget, and timeframe.

Look for the facts behind the generalities. "If the brochure says, "We bring in buying teams from the largest companies", we need to ask for examples of the types of companies, and ask for the titles of the people who will make up those buying teams.

Scrutinize Public Shows, too. Although public shows don't use the computerized registration systems that are common at trade shows, demographic data can still be captured. Most trade show management tend to utilize surveys that allow them to learn attendees' ages, household income, distance traveled to the show, reason for attending, areas of interest, and purchase intentions.

What do previous exhibitors think of the show? The experience of exhibitors from companies that are similar in size to your company, or in the same industry (if we can talk to them), can help us to determine what to expect if we exhibited. The following are additional questions within this area to be asked:

- Ask show management for the names and phone numbers of contacts at such companies.
- Ask previous exhibitors if they saw the kinds of buyers they needed to see. Did they make sales at the show? Or can they trace subsequent sales to the show? Is the show important in its industry? Is it keeping up with industry developments? Did management work with exhibitors to help them have the best show possible?

Will management target the audience that is right for your company? Will direct mail and ads be aimed at the people you want to reach? Your company will need Trade Show management to tell you what they're planning to do to promote the event. Several trade show management companies prepare a year in advance by listing trade show publications they will use and their circulation, the number of ads they will run in each, the number of news releases they will send and when, and the number of mailings they will do and to whom.

What are public show plans? Because many people learn about public shows only from advertising, these plans are key. Your company will need to know how much radio advertising will be done, on which radio stations, how much TV, how much print. Usually the features addressed in the advertising indicate what type of audience is being targeted.

What do previous attendees think of the show? Attendees know better than management if a show is growing or declining. Show management should be willing to provide names and phone numbers of previous attendees. Call at least 10 past attendees and ask the following key questions:

- How much time did you spend at the show?
- Did you go more than one day?
- Did you urge others to go?
- Did they see the new products they wanted to see?
- As a result of visiting the show did they or will they purchase anything?
- What would they like to see at the show and what was missing?

How will management promote this show? Show management should have specific plans for reaching a carefully targeted audience, and should be willing to share those plans with prospective exhibitors. Will direct mail ads be aimed at the people you want to reach?

How will management help attendees to find your company? For professional, reputable show management, the overriding concern will be to bring buyer and seller together. You will need to determine before the show opens if the attendees can pre-register and thus enter the show more quickly. You will have to determine if the show guide is sent in advance and is the floor plan easy to read and color-coded. At the show you will need to determine if there are computer terminals that help attendees locate specific products and may even print Lists of companies with booth numbers. In addition you need to be assured of non conflict between seminars and the exhibit hours.

Trade Show Activity Guide

The following is the recommended timetable approach for all types of trade show events. This method of advanced planning will give you better control and the opportunity to end up with more impressive results:

Trade Show Logistics

6 – 12 Months In Advance

- Plan Budget
- Select Shows
- Book Space

4 Months Prior to each show

- Determine show objectives and investigate and evaluate show audience.
- Create marketing message
- Obtain kit and read carefully
- Start determination of what graphics will be used with the show.
- Start assigning sales staff -(utilize most appropriate sales and technical people).

3 Months Prior to each Show

- Establish work schedule
- Make travel plans/book hotel rooms
- Set-up any needed outside suppliers
- Plan printed materials
- Create pre and post show promotional pieces

6 - 8 weeks Prior to each show

- Confirm staff recruiting and distribute company and show information
- Check of status of display materials
- Order product samples, literature, etc. from within company
- Order necessary show services

3 - 4 weeks prior to a Show

- Write and mail customers (targets) invitation letter (with incentive draw to booth)
- and finalize any VIP guest events
- Alert Press and Media of any Press Conference
- Arrange any necessary Pre-show promotions (Trade/Industry Publications, Local
- Publications, Billboards, Association Newsletters, Local Radio/ television)
- Confirm shipping information and provide to vendors
- Prepare training materials for staff at the show
- Prepare Press release Packets for local and trade publications. Product and/or service
- Applications articles and personal invitations to trade/local editors.

1 - 2 Weeks prior to a Show

- Collect supplies, tickets, service orders sent to show in advance
- Bring credit cards for payment on site (doesn't really apply)

At Show Before Opening

- Travel to site, pick up badges, assemble display
- Confirm arrival of display, equipment, literature and supervise set-up
- Conduct pre-show briefing and outline goals
- Provide Press kits for the Press Office
- Have Reprints of articles as giveaways

During the Show

- Conduct daily meetings to assess progress and process leads
- Make arrangements to dismantle our display
- Reserve next year's space

- Transmit sales leads to our office for preparation of mail packages to attendees

After the Show

- Distribute and follow up on sales leads and orders
- Send thank you letters to visitors and company employees
- Prepare a thorough evaluation of our show participation

Trade Show Floor Basics

The most crucial aspect of any exhibit is your people. Your image does not stop with an elaborate display, fancy advertising or impressive literature. These certainly help, but it will be your people who sell you company and your products and services. The teams you choose at each show are your ambassadors.

It will be these individuals who make or break relationships with attendees. Your personnel will need to be *Enthusiastic, Observant*, have excellent *Product* knowledge are keen *Listeners*, are *Empathetic* to the visitor's situations. The training will be essential for a unified effort on the trade show floor. In particular your booth duty.

Why your company is exhibiting. The purpose for your involvement in the show and what we you are expecting to achieve through participation. Every show should have a targeted goal.

What you are exhibiting. Each show has its own personality and target market. You need to make clear what products/services you plan to exhibit. There must be no surprises when your team arrives at the display.

What you expect from them. Your selected team for each show must be encouraged to select their own goals based on overall exhibiting goals, They also need to know what you expect them to do on a daily basis (*this is critical*!). For example, how many prospects do you expect them to interact with and what kind of information do you want them to gather.

How to do what you expect from them. You must train your representatives to be more effective on the show room floor. You will need to show them how to talk about the product/programs/services displayed and to effectively qualify prospects. I know this sounds irrational since we assume that a salesperson know this; however, trade shows have their own set of rules of engagement and guidelines.

To keep everyone on track, you will need to meet with your team regularly, before the show begins and at the end of the day. You will need to remind them what needs to be accomplished, evaluate performance, answer questions, monitor goals and generally keep everyone motivated.

I am recommending that you take a few minutes at the end of each day to debrief the day's activities and look at ways to improve your performance the following day.

Guidelines for Engaging Prospects

The following are a series of actions that should guide your activities on the trade show floor:

- Prepare 3 –6 engaging questions before the show.
- Create the right impression, smile and maintain eye contact
- Encourage visitors to want to spend time with you.
- Be friendly and non-threatening to build rapport
- Ask open-ended questions – beginning with who, what, where, when, why or how. Relate questions to the attendees industry, product/service and its benefits to a specific situation.
- Practice, practice, practice

Guidelines for Qualifying Visitors.

- Remember the 80/20 Rule: 80% of the time listen to visitors, 20% of the time talk about our programs/services, and never talk for more than 2 minutes straight.

- Ask questions which reveal their level of interest/need for our programs/services.
- Inquire into their decision making process, i.e., the prospects influence or authority in the buying decision.
- Explore time and budget parameters

Guidelines for Sales Literature

- You should not hand out expensive literature. 64% of the literature handed out at shows is thrown away. Instead you need an inexpensive, maybe cute and clever tri-fold to go. Other recent statistics quote only 10% of all literature handed out actually find its way back to the prospects office.
- Offer to send information. You will need to send literature in a timely manner. It should be on the prospect's desk within 48 hours of the show.
- Only give literature to qualified prospects!

Guidelines for Premiums

- You will need to get some qualifying information from visitors before handing over a gift; however most gifts will be linked to a pre show mailer to a target audience of prospects whom we are trying to have visit you during the show.
- The gift will be used as a "thank you" for stopping.

Guidelines for Presenting

- You will use the FBI formula (feature/benefit/inclination, e.g. "Our incentive programs (feature) will help to boost employee and field sales productivity (benefit)
- Do you feel this program would satisfy the need for getting improved employee and sales productivity?
- Let prospects know how your products/programs/services compare with the competition (after all the competitors are doing the same).
- Show existing customers new products/programs/services.

Guidelines for Closing

- Change body position, minimize eye contact and shake hands.
- Communicate your follow-up action plan.

Embarrassing Obvious Common Sense Tips

Unfortunately, salespeople are not as well disciplined, as we would like at trade show so I have compiled the "Holy Book" of Obviousness for them to follow:

- Rehearse the sales pitch and do a live demonstration beforehand.
- Don't sit, read, smoke, eat or drink in the exhibit.
- Avoid drinking alcohol or eating garlicky or spicy foods during the day.
- Dress in a conservative business-like manner or one notch better than your visitors.
- Wear very comfortable shoes
- Arrive at the exhibit as least 15 minutes before you scheduled time and complete your paperwork before you leave.
- Let your fellow colleagues know when you leave the exhibit.
- Refrain from using the telephone in the exhibit while visitors are around (no cellular especially).
- Avoid crossing your arms while talking to prospects.
- Keep a reduced, photocopied product price list of past proposals in your pocket for easy reference.
- Write down as much prospect information for follow-up.
- Get lots of rest and exercise as shows can drain your energy level.

Lead Management

One of the biggest after-show frustrations companies have is quantifying and managing leads gathered. More often than not, leads are distributed to the sales force and little if anything is seen or heard of the outcome. Show performance and ROI is difficult, if not impossible to measure. The following is the recommended plan of approach that will help us produce measurable and profitable trade show leads.

Review your show goals

You will need to set specific goals for each show and to be totally clear on what it is you want to achieve through our participation at the various shows you attend. Knowing what results you want is critical in the data gathering process.

Plan a questioning strategy.

Prior to the events, you will need to set a plan of questions to ask prospects to ensure we get the information needed.

Designing a customized lead card

Design a lead card that records all the information needed to follow up with prospects after the show. It will be user-friendly with boxes to check.

Establish and use a prospect ranking system.

Establish a ranking system and determine how immediate is their need for your programs/services. Are they likely to purchase within a month or Year? For example 1 = immediate, 2 = interested in buying within the next 6 Months, 3 = partial interest.

Conduct a debriefing session.

At the end of each show day and before leads are sent off for the team. Hot Leads will be shared with the team. This will give the other team members the opportunity to add any further information that may help the follow up.

Establish a lead-handling plan.

Prior to the show participation you will establish how leads will be handled. You will Need to assign an individual the responsibility of collecting all hot leads at the end of Each day and overnight them to your office for immediate processing.

Develop a follow up system.

Based on your ranking of leads you will need to follow up within 3-5 days after a Show.

Using a computer for tracking.

Utilize a computer to help establish a lead tracking system.

Make your salespeople accountable for the leads.

Salesperson's need to be accountable for leads given to them. Every month they need tol submit a written update to the Trade Show Manager. Any salesperson not conforming to the lead reports should not receive future leads.

Measuring Results

Leads need to be measured against projected ROI expectations and an in depth analysis will be performed after each trade show event has occurred.

Trade Show Themes

There are a lot of themes for trade shows and there are just as many companies from trade show booth developers to Advertising Agencies that will be more than glad to help you develop themes. Below are a few ideas to give you some concepts Remember you are only limited by your imagination.

#1: RACECAR concept

"Gentlemen, Start Your Engines"

Your logo would dominant on all pieces.

Mailer #1 could be a 4/C; A-6 mailer. It would be a clean, graphic with a sound chip of a motor racing as you open the card. Card would include all the show information. The race car would be Number "X" and have your company logo on the hood. The call-to-action will be incentive based . . . a chance to win a free NASCAR weekend trip or tickets to "pro-driving school". A special mailer could also be sent to 30-40 of your company's key customers to invite them to "special event at the Texas Motor Speedway" (all expenses included).

Mailer #2 could be a small checkered flag with your company logo printed in black/red swoosh. The flag should be rolled and placed in a small tube for mailing to increase interest and stand out from all the clutter. Message would be "your flag has your 'starting position'; please visit us at booth #XXX to see how you've placed". All flags win a premium item and one flag wins a large item. All get to enter to win trip.

Booth Decor: Racing flags in green, white, yellow, mostly red and checkered. Ball caps, t-shirts, key chains, etc. Attire could be racing shirts.

Premium Items: Possibilities include car shades, sunglasses, driving gloves, flags, hot wheel cars with your company logo, small tool kits, NASCAR rain ponchos or seat cushions, imprinted stop watches, license plates, racing lapel pins, windshield ice scraper (cold weather), race car keychain, checkered flag note pads, etc.

Press Kits/ Editorial Marketing: Racing theme in nature, the press kit would offer a premium of a greater value to the key customers. i.e. leather racing gloves or car mats.

#2: SPORTS concept (baseball)

"Home Run with your company", "It's your turn at bat with your company", without your company on your team, you could strike out".

Mailer #1 could be in the shape of a baseball diamond with a small package of peanuts enclosed. Each peanut bag could have a code print on them; bring your bag, match the code at our "home plate" (booth) and win a prize. Or you could enclose an empty company printed popcorn bag. You would have to bring the bag to booth to fill up with free popcorn and chance to win a prize. No popcorn bags available at booth; attendees have to bring mailed bag.

Mailer #2 reinforces same concept. Could include a "game ticket" with seat/section number printed. Match your stadium seat number identified at the booth to win a weekend trip to the World Series. Win your company baseball caps through the same idea.

Booth Décor/Giveaways/Press Kits: baseballs, baseball jerseys, baseball caps with your company logo, peanuts, hot dogs, popcorn machine, Pepsi machine, team pennants, ink pens shaped like baseball bats or miniature "little sluggers". Key customers could be gathered and taken out for a night at a local baseball game.

#3 WILD, WILD WEST concept (cowboy)

"Okay, partner, mosey on over to Booth #XX", use your company logo on a Branding Iron. "Our brand is a mark of quality"

Mailer #1: You could have a branding iron made with your company logo and actually stamp onto a leather square to adhere to a mailer that has been tea stained to look old and worn like from the 1800s.

Mailer #2: reinforce with a "shot-up wanted poster with the branding-iron X mark". You're "Wanted" at Booth #XXX for a wild, wild time. Key customers could be invited to a hoedown at Billy Bob's complete with a full-out BBQ dinner.

Booth Décor/ Giveaways/ Press Kits: cowboy hats, western boot-shaped desk weights, your company printed handkerchiefs, tin cups with your company logo, boot-shaped cups.

#4 TEXAS RANGERS concept (lawman)

Similar to Wild, Wild West concept but more towards the law enforcers of the 20th century. "Your company. We're the Good Guys in the White Hats". "Our company is here to Save the Day".

Mailer #1: Could have a Cowboy Hat Bands printed with the your company logo, put white hats on our booth staff working at the show and then photograph them and include as the main graphic element of the mailer. Fun concept with face recognition. "Meet the Good Guys in the White Hats."

Mailer #2: Could be a miniature pistol (like on a keychain) or a target practice/shooting range "dummy outline". Try your luck at shooting up the bad guys at Booth #XX to win a prize.

Booth Décor/ Giveaways/ Press Kits: tin star badges with your company logo. Hat bands, western shirts, handkerchiefs, or a dartboard where the "guns" shoot suction cup darts. Hit different parts of the board to win different prizes. Key customers could be gathered for an evening at a location with a western theme.

CHAPTER 5
HOW TO IMPLEMENT A SEMINAR SUCCESSFULLY

Why Do A Seminar

Everyone at some time or another wants to do a seminar to grow business. Here are some reasons why people go through the pain and expense to produce seminars.

- To create awareness of your company seminar programs on a regional and national level.
- To differentiate your company from your competitors by publicizing unique value-added services, product knowledge through direct sales, agent channels and interconnect channel.
- To provide professionals, including current and prospective customers, with educational forums that will allow them to become more productive in their own careers.
- To position your company as a resource that provides information on current issues and topics facing business professionals.

The primary objective in developing seminar programs is to customize topics that will apply to specific market segments or that will cross over to multiple market segments.

Sample Seminar Program Budget

The following are suggested cost items for implementation of a seminar program:

ITEM	COSTS
Promotion	
Direct Mail	1,000.00
Graphic design	500.00
Printing	1000.00
Postage	1000.00
Sales/Support Materials	
Brochures	1,000.00
Program Schedules	100.00
200 Page Workbooks in binders (100 sets)	1,000.00
Certificate of Completion	100.00
Name Badges	50.00
Table Tents	50.00
Database Design and Management	
Contact Lists	2,000.00
Telemarketing	
Confirmation/Follow up	TBD
Promotional Merchandise	
Folders	100.00
Pens	100.00
Mugs	100.00
Exhibit Materials	
Seminar Banner	100.00
Easel and Flip Chart	50.00
Facility	
Meeting Room	300.00
Catering Breaks (2) coffee + sweets	200.00
Audio Visual Equipment	
Computer for Power Point presentation	200.00
Sound Equipment	50.00
Electricity Hook ups	50.00
Lights	0

Outlets for lap tops	0
Travel Expenses	
Speakers Travel	1,000.00
Transportation	
Shuttle Service	0
Taxi Service	0
Hotel Accommodations	
Speakers Room and Board	500.00
Speakers Fees	0
TOTALS	**$10,550.00**

Seminar Payment by Attendees

Charging for seminars programs creates value. If you select not to charge a fee, the prospects may determine that your seminar programs do not provide inherent value or are not worth their time (away from the office) especially if travel is required.

I began teaching over 100 seminars for INC Magazine from 1980 – 1985 and charged $495.00 for one-day seminars and $795.00 for two-day seminars. In 1988 I introduced one-day $99.00 seminars for Grant Thornton in Chicago, St. Louis and Philadelphia for the same topics as the INC Magazine seminars.

Using a 10,000 brochure mailing my capture rate was ½ of 1% or 50 attendees per seminar. The payout was about 3-4 clients acquired or $100,000 in consulting revenues.

Seminar Locations

Once the location has been selected to hold the seminars, a specific site within each city will need to be chosen. In most cases, seminars are held in a hotel meeting facilities. The advantage of utilizing a hotel is that they are experienced in handling required reservations for meeting functions. Important questions to ask when considering a hotel or facility for seminars should include:

- Has the hotel/facility planned for any construction during your seminar date?
- What events are going to be taking place in the room(s) next to yours?
- Does the hotel/facility use its own audio/video equipment, or do you rent it especially for the event?
- Directions to the hotel from the airports and freeways

Booking Meeting Rooms

Generally, if a hotel books a lot of business, it is going to have what is called book-out policies. This is usually the case in major metropolitan areas (e.g. Chicago, Seattle). At these hotels the main incentive is to book sleeping rooms; meeting rooms are kind of incidental. This means that meeting rooms are generally held for big groups that book large blocks of rooms for guests.

If a substantial number of rooms are not booked, the hotel generally will not release the meeting space. In smaller cities, hotels will generally take the booking six months in advance regardless if rooms are reserved for the seminar. Actual costs may vary substantially from hotel to hotel. On average, meeting rooms can range from $500 to $1500 or more per day. Refreshments during breaks are usually extra.

Facility Comparison Sheet

The following are items that require comparison when selecting a seminar location:

- Facility Name
- Location
- Address
- City
- State
- Zip Code
- Telephone

- Fax
- Facility/Banquet Manager Name
- Distance from Airport
- Confirmation/Dates
- Availability
- Information Requested
- Conference Facility Rates
- Deposit Required
- AV Equipment Availability
- Accommodation Rates
- Group Discounts
- Catering
- Banquets Areas/Rooms
- Site Inspection

Industry Events

In addition to developing stand-alone seminar programs, piggybacking seminars with current industry events will help to drive-up attendance. Two types of industry events include industry trade shows and association meetings. It may be prudent for you to identify key associations in the seminar cities and solicit their support for your event.

Seminar Moderator A seminar moderator is a key component for your event. Pick someone with good public speaking skills and the ability to be intuitive with the audience. In addition some of this individual's on site responsibilities will include:

- Check-In (Name Badges, Workbooks, etc.)
- Welcome Remarks
- Introducing Speakers
- Scheduling Breaks
- Moderate Question and Answer Sessions

- Monitor Program Schedule
- Seminar Surveys
- On-site coordination with Facility Manager (Room Layout, Catering, etc)

Attendance Goals

You should be seeking 30-50 attendees per seminar to justify a Return on Investment .

Equipment

Equipment Requirements will vary by seminar size, budget and/or the speaker presenting the information.

Audio

Hand held microphone (or) clip microphone attached to presenter's shirt.

Visual

- Flip Charts
- Chalkboard
- Dry-Erase Marker Board
- DVD Player
- Video Television Monitors
- LCD Projectors
- Laptop computer for Power Point Presentation
- Laser Pointer

Hotels within medium to large size cities have convention services departments that supply everything from registration tables to lecterns. We will need to verify what equipment is included in the meeting/banquet room rental agreement. If the hotel does not supply the required audio/visual, then a local audio visual company will be used.

Web Promotion

Once you have outlined and established your seminar you will need to establish a ur web site for registration and payment collection. Once you have produced several seminars you will be able to extract video content and also place parts of it on your web site for future promotions of seminars.

Seminar Materials

Each seminar should require the following supplies and/or materials:

- Seminar Registration Forms
- Badges
- Table Tents (Attendee Name and Company)
- Confirmation Forms
- Program/Direct Mail Brochures
- Signs/Banners
- Pop UP Booth Display
- Workbooks
- Certificates of Completion
- Evaluation Forms
- Thank You Follow-Up Letters

One cost effective approach when designing seminar promotion materials is to use pre-printed shells that can quickly customized for a specific seminar topic or event. The materials can be over-printed in black with the speakers(s) name, seminar topics, dates, times, location, etc.

Seminar Registration Form & Information Packet

Once the speaker(s) has/have been selected and confirmed for a specific seminar date, a registration form and information packet will be mailed to the appropriate target audience to solicit attendance. The packet will include general information on the seminar program, speaker(s) biography, location date, time, travel/hotel accommodations and program cost. The packet will include a seminar registration from, with a response date, for the recipient to complete and return to (your company) (seminar coordinator).

Confirmation Letter

A confirmation letter will need to be sent to those individuals who register and pay for a seminar program. The letter will confirm receipt of payment, date, time & location the event, directions to the facility, transportation information, and hotel registration (if required).

Signs/Banners

Signs and banners are required to assist with the promotion and branding of the (your company) seminars. Signs will be used at the registration table, literature table, on easels and banners will be used for each seminar program.

Workbooks

Workbooks will be used for each seminar. The workbook will encompass all presentations. The workbook will be graphically synergistic with the overall seminar program. They will highlight the speaker's key points and provide space for notes and additional information recorded by the participants. The workbooks will include the corporate address and 800# with seminar presenters names and telephone numbers. Participants can contact (your company) if they are interested in future seminar programs or out network services. The workbooks will present a professional image while working within the budget parameters previously established.

Evaluations

Another important item to include in the materials distributed to seminar attendees (participants) is an evaluation from. This one page evaluation form can be handed out during registration, inserted into the workbook, or passed out to the participants at the end of the program.

The evaluation form will include questions on the following:

- Number of speakers for the program

- The program schedule
- The price of the program
- Its length and start time
- The strength of the speakers
- Topics attendees would like to see included in the future
- Additional Comments

In addition, the evaluation form will include a rating scale of 1-5 (1-Poor, 5-Excellent)

- Session meets the objectives stated
- Topic relevant to you and your business
- Content of the presentation
- Overall speaker effectiveness
- Audio Visual presentation
- Handout materials support the presentation

All questions will be easy to answer and will provide attendees the option of not providing their names and addresses. This option encourages candid responses. Individuals are more likely to write negative comments if they can do so anonymously.

Thank You Letters

After each seminar program send a follow-up thank you letter.

Sales Leads

Leads will need to be tracked to determine seminar effectiveness

CHAPTER 6
HOW TO PROMOTE YOUR BUSINESS WITH LITTLE OR NO MONEY

Business Promotion Tips

Research your market before committing to any promotion. What may be good for someone else may not work for you.

Plan your promotions. Don't just throw together advertising and hope for the best. Develop promotions which take advantage of seasonal and economic changes. What worked last year may not work today, and what works today may not work tomorrow.

Evaluate your promotional program periodically. Get rid of some of the less successful promotions and replace them with other programs you feel will produce better results.

Follow the lead of the major corporations and distribute your promotional dollars between several different promotions. In small businesses this usually means 5 – 10 different promotions.

Develop promotions which communicate to the prospect what you can do to help them with their need or want. Entice prospects by offering a free estimate, special, trial period, money back guarantee, buy 1 get 1 free etc.

Budget a specific percent (%) of your projected gross income to promotion. In most businesses this averages to about 10%. In new businesses (i.e. businesses less than 3 years old) these averages to about 15%.

Have a realistic idea of what a successful promotion is. Many businesses expect a $10,000 return off a $500 investment or a new customer who will spend $50 per month for the next year.

Compare promotions like any other investment, by the percent (%) of return. Don't expect $500 of print advertising to bring in the same amount of new business as $5,000 of radio or television advertising.

Change ad copy periodically. Different messages appeal to different customers.

Develop a habit of determining where new business is coming from. A good tracking system would allow the employees to distinguish what promotion the customer was responding to.

Getting New Business

Turn you ex employer into your client: Your former employer already knows your capability and has a proven need for it. Sometimes you can negotiate to do a contractual basis what you had been doing full-time, or you can negotiate a contract to train your replacement.

Subcontract or do overload: Your competitors can be an excellent source of business. Statistics have found that 11% to 21% of new businesses come from the competition.

Work as a temporary in the field in which you will be doing business: Working for a temporary agency can provide invaluable experience and excellent contacts. At the same time it provides a flexible source of income while building your business.

Make an offer they can't refuse: Identify people who need your skills and make them a special offer they can't refuse. Be sure you cover all your costs and ask them to serve as a reference for you in the future.

Volunteer: Sometimes this kind of work begets work. Volunteer efforts can be a source of experience and reference that you can use for getting future business.

Join clubs and associations: People like to buy from people with whom they are familiar. You can make a lot of friends when you join clubs and associations. If you join with the idea of serving the club or committees the members will appreciate your devotion. Joining clubs and associations provides many benefits:

- You meet a lot of prospects.
- You meet a lot of referrers
- You have access to other company's grapevines
- You can become a friend with honest prospects and customers

Cultivating Client Relationships

Don't forget who pays the bills. Your customers pay the bills by bringing you business, and it's because of them you stay in business. Focus on your customers and obtain their feedback. Listen to what they have to say and use their suggestions to improve your business plans. Keep customers coming back by:

- Delivering exceptional quality
- Providing outstanding service
- Establishing a reputation of reliability

Don't Promise what you can't deliver: The opportunity to work with a large corporation may cause you to make promises you may not be able to keep. Be realistic and check your schedule and workload to determine if you have time to complete the job. And don't forget to consider if you are the right person to handle the project.

Go the Extra Mile: Provide added touches to your customer's project, known as "value added services"/ enhancing your services does not always involve money. Your time is valuable and offering more of it , exceeding the client's expectations and therefore leading to another project.

Make it Easy for Clients to Do Business with You. You may provide a necessary service, but how easy is it for people to do business with you?

Do you have consistent business hours? Do you miss several phone calls during the day? If you are not available when prospects call, you may lose valuable business.

Promise Your Clients Business: When you work with clients for a long time, you become very familiar with their business. If you believe they are good at what they do, share it with others. Tell people about your clients, and how they may help others.

Make a Commitment to Customer Satisfaction: If you assume that your clients are satisfied and that they will automatically call you if they need anything, you could be wrong. As your client base continues to grow, it is most important that you maintain the same level of service you provided when you first earned your client's business. Then look for ways to improve.

Send a Business Anniversary Card: Pull yourself out of the holiday card game with the exception of sending business anniversary cards. Remember the first meeting you had with each client and take the time to send a card to celebrate the date. The client will be flattered that you remembered. Write a note letting the client know that you are looking forward to working together for many more years.

Designing Promotional Materials

Your promotional materials are the corridor into the minds of buyers. What you are striving for is a "Top of Mind" experience.

Once you have established your identity in a "design image" keep it consistent throughout all your materials: The image you are establishing is like a photo or a blueprint. You want to expose to every level of your business so buyers begin to associate your image and your identity with:

- Business Cards
- Letterhead
- Second Sheets

- Envelopes
- Mailing Labels
- Brochures
- Websites (SEO)
- E-Commerce
- Flyers
- Post Cards
- Price Lists
- Newsletters
- Invoices
- Presentation Packages
- Handouts (key chains)

Business Cards

One way to make your business look successful are creative business cards:

Basic cards: This is a good card style when utility is all you need. It's a no-nonsense approach that can appeal to clients and prospects who would not be impressed by fancy design features--the people who want "just the facts, ma'am." The design is simple, and the information is clear and concise. A basic card is usually printed in black ink on plain white or cream stock.

Picture cards: Having your face on your card--whether it's a photograph, a drawing or a caricature--helps a contact remember you the next time she sees you. Images representing a product or services, or a benefit your business provides, can help you communicate your business better than dozens of words. Color is often helpful on a picture card, too.

Tactile cards: Some cards are distinguished not so much by how they look as by how they feel. They may use nonstandard materials, such as metal or wood, or have unusual shapes, edges, folds or embossing.

Tactile cards tend to be considerably more expensive than regular cards because they use nonstandard production processes such as die cuts.

Multipurpose cards: A card can do more than promote your name and business--it can also serve as a discount coupon, an appointment reminder or some other function. It may also provide valuable information that the average person may need. For example, a hotel may include a map on the back of its card for any guests who are walking around the vicinity. A card of any type can be made multipurpose by adding these types of features.

Outside-the-box cards: A wildly original, fanciful or extravagant presentation can draw extra attention. Creativity knows no bounds--except the amount of money you wish to spend. I've seen examples of these types of cards that were made of chocolate or that folded out into a miniature box to keep small items in. One of the most notable was a dentist's card that included a small compartment for dental floss to be pulled out.

10 Networking Tips for using Business Cards

- Never leave home without them. Before leaving home, your checklist should be expanded to include your business cards. Any 'per chance' meeting is an opportunity to give out a business card. A morning run or a quick trip to the local store could be an opportunity to network.
- Insert a business card when mailing bill payments. You may not think a person in South Dakota who opens your credit card bill payment can help you. Never underestimate the power of networking.
- Use proper business card etiquette. Whenever you give a business card, ask for a business card. When given a business card, don't just take it and place it in your pocket. Make the person feel important by looking at their card for a few seconds. Write comments on the card such as date, location and common points of interest.

- Be generous. Give business cards out to everyone, including family and friends. Don't let vanity stop you from giving out your last business card or giving 2 at a time to each person. I have met many people who have totally missed the purpose of a business card. I once asked a person for a second business card, so I could refer his services. His response was "I only have a few cards left and I need them", as he looked again at his name on the card. Hoarding your business cards only makes your wallet feel full, not your bank account.
- Ask for referrals. When giving a business card you should ask, "I would appreciate a referral, if you know anyone that could use my services". People naturally like to do favors for people. This places you in a good position with them and they will feel better about helping you. Give them 2 cards.
- Maximize every "per chance" meeting. You never know when you might meet someone who can help you. Family or friends' social events could produce unexpected encounters with people. Don't discount those events.
- Place yourself at the right place at the right time. Consider volunteering to help out at the job fair or other types of events. This puts you in a better strategic position for presenting your resume or business card. Company representatives might view you differently, if they know you are willing to go the extra mile in helping them make their presence easier to manage.
- Use "In Your Face" follow up. Did you ever have a job interview and wonder why they never called you back? Today's economic climate dictates you might be competing with 20, 50, 100 or more other people for the same position. So it's up to you to give a person a reason to call you back. Immediately after a meeting sends a hand written note thanking the person for their time. Insert your business card. Now you're in the driver's seat in standing out from other people.
- Use promotions to promote YOU, Inc. Consider getting some blank greeting cards. Search the internet to find out the address of the company's executive offices. Send the blank card with a hand written note sincerely congratulating a person

on their promotion. Insert your business card. You have just made someone's day and may create an impression that makes a person feel compelled to respond back to you.

- Brand yourself with a slogan. Print a slogan on your business card that answers the question "Why should I hire you" Or "What makes you different from everyone else?" A catchy phrase or slogan makes all the difference between getting hired or not, because people will remember you long after a meeting.

Flyers

Flyers are an inexpensive way to promote your business, products, services and events. They are a wonderful, not to mention effective, marketing tool for new business start-ups as well as more established businesses with budgetary constraints. Business flyers can be used just about anywhere; bookstores, parking lots, under doors, on counters, in store windows, bars, restaurants, baseball fields, bulletin boards, light poles, where ever your target market is—you can promote yourself. It's completely up to you.

Inexpensive

Have you looked at the cost of placing even a small space ad in the local paper? It's probably higher than you'd expect. Flyers, on the other hand, give you more space and freedom to describe your product or service at length and can be produced for a relatively small fee.

A strategically focused and to-the-point business flyer will catch the attention of prospective customers. And a well-designed business flyer is equivalent to your target market perusing a full-page Ad Now that's effective.Flyers aren't just for advertising garage sales anymore, although they are great for that too. Flyers can be used in so many ways it's easy to lose track. Here are some examples of the many professionally designed and effective flyers:

- Film Festival Flyer Design
- Special Promotion Flyer Design
- Product Sales Flyer Design

- Grand Opening Announcement Flyer Design
- Weekend Sales Event Flyer Design
- Concert Flyer Design
- Fund-Raising Flyer Design
- Flyer Designs for Auctions
- New Home Sales Flyer Design
- Real Estate Development Flyer Design
- Sales Coupons Flyer Design
- Limited Availability Products
- Real Estate Marketing Flyer Design
- Highlight Sheets Flyer Design
- Listing Presentations
- Store Specials and Promotions
- Folder Inserts
- Selling Boats, Cars, Hang Gliders, etc.

Flyer Rules

Tell people how you will solve their problems, Focus on Benefits, Make an offer they can't refuse and show that others value your service

Business Brochure

A brochure is a pamphlet usually consisting of one sheet of paper printed on both sides and folded two or three times. The following are reasons for developing brochures

- Explain who you are
- Tell what you do, how you benefit the community
- Show that supports and endorses you
- Provide a graphic identification for you (a logo or symbol)
- Attract new persons to your events and activities
- Provide information to employees about programs, etc

- Promote a product

3-30-3 Test

When designing a brochure, use the 3 second, 30 second, 3 minutes test to see how well it will work:

- Will they catch someone's interest for 3 seconds?
- Will they induce the person to read on for 30 seconds?
- Will they get the person to read for 3 minutes?
- Knowing that 30 seconds is the average amount of time someone will spend on your literature, have you designed it to be effective in that time?

Newsletter

The most important aspect of creating a successful newsletter is the market. You need to research who will buy the subscription and how much they are willing to pay. But there are sound methods of testing the market to assure you come out ahead and establish yourself in the field. If you have a special interest that has a broad following, you might find that a newsletter will be readily accepted and flourish.

What Is A Newsletter?

A newsletter is a special timely report on a single subject. It is a personalized, concise statement from an expert or person thoroughly familiar with a specialized field. Newsletters are maintained solely by subscriptions; there is no advertising. Most are printed within low budget means, typewritten, from two to eight pages. The specialized information in newsletters is current, and usually cannot be found elsewhere. They are a logical extension to trade journals and magazines. Aimed at a select group, they often contain the inside information in the field, hot tips or news scoops that become old news in publications of the trade.

Why Are Newsletters Popular?

The focus of the newsletter is success. Success in business, success in hobbies, success in health and happiness. The information contained in the newsletters motivates readers to follow the advice. What are the best investments? Where are the trade shows? How can I get an edge on winning contests?

There is an endless need for specific knowledge in every field of endeavor. Since there is a high standard of competition within every aspect of our modern life, people search for ways to be in the know, and use that information effectively.

One of the reasons subscription prices can stay high is because people are paying for the knowledge and what might be gained by it. If a two hundred dollar newsletter saves a company thousands of dollars in excellent advice, then it is well worth the price.

What It Takes

The topic you choose has got to be your major interest. You'll be living with it day in and day out for years, so you need to be devoted to the subject. Usually, it's not hard. You probably already have a chosen field of endeavor, or have developed a keen interest in a special hobby or sport. Writing a newsletter is only one more way to demonstrate your interest.

Read any newsletters you can find. What do they talk about? How much do they cost? How long have they been in business? You might want to talk to the publishers of a few to find out how they started and what troubles they encountered. Consider paying them a consulting fee to help you get on your way.

Take a look at all the trade magazines of the topic you'd like to work with. Find out if there are any newsletters already existing in that field. But don't worry - there is usually room for more if you keep to another aspect of the business or endeavor.

Keep up with the current trends in health, money, sports, or social events and styles. What's new with the young people? Or the elderly? There are many retired people actively pursuing hundreds of various interests. How can you tap into that market?

What To Call It

The title at the top of the newsletter is the most visual aspect of the publication. It reflects the content and it reflects you.

Style And Format

A low-budget newsletter is usually one column, typewritten copy, with ample but not wide margins. Anything with two or more columns should be typeset, which is an extra expense you don't need.

The most economical way of printing the newsletter is on one or two 11 x 17 inch pages, printed on both sides, and folded. This will give you a small booklet of four to eight pages, each the standard 8 1/2 x 11 inch size.

You might consider having it three-hole punched. It doesn't cost much to have this done at the printers, and it could be an added feature to encourage subscribers to save the valuable information.

Any graphics should be kept simple, but don't be afraid to use subheads to break up the copy. A few words capitalized or in a larger or darker print help the reader identify the information, and make it easier to read.

Keep enough white space to encourage reading, but fill the pages to make the subscriber feel the newsletter fulfills its promises.

What To Include

Consider a copy format that is divided by types of information. For example, you can have a section labeled profiles, another on upcoming events. Perhaps you have a calendar of shows, conventions, or seminars that would concern readers.

Finding The Facts

Your first few issues won't lack for information, because you already have pages of information to publish. But after that, you'll need renewable sources of copy.

What's new in the industry? Your associates and colleagues are the prime source of undercurrents in the field you write about. Renew and make new contacts - they'll be invaluable for getting information.

Writing Copy

In this publication, you are the authority. Use strong, direct statements with an active voice. Although you are often offering opinion, the content should be factual.

Your readers are intelligent, and experts in the same field you are writing about. You'll need to back up your statements with research. A rule of thumb is that three concurring sources make fact.

Getting Ready For Printing

Once you have all your copy finished, you need to have it type set. Spend the money necessary for the final copy to be letter perfect. Any errors will reflect on you - even typographical errors.

The first few newsletters you publish will require a lot of trial and error with copy and layout. You'll need to decide how many spaces to leave between the end of a paragraph and the beginning of a subhead, how many spaces to indent, and how big the margins will be.

Think about what is important to the format. Some newsletters use italics or underlined words to emphasize the importance. And some overuse these methods. Always let good taste dictate the layout and style of your publication.

When a whole line is taken up by a few words, or the last half of a hyphenated word, it is called a widow. These look sloppy in any type of publication, so you will want to rewrite the paragraph to extend or shorten that sentence.

Be careful about carry-overs to the next page. It's very awkward to hyphenate at the bottom of a page, or have only one line at the top of the next, then space for a subhead. As you get more adept at preparing copy, you'll be able to write to fit. And the looks will improve.

The basic standard for a newsletter is clarity. Can you read the type? Are the ideas well presented and easy to understand? Do the subheads interest and motivate the readers?

The final typed copy is exactly what will be printed. Since photo offset is the least expensive way to print multiple copies of typewritten material, the pages must be clean.

Any second color should be indicated with an overlay. This is a sheet of tracing paper taped to the copy with printer's instructions written on it and sections circled that need special attention. For the first year of publication, you won't need to put in any photos - in fact, you may never use photos. But give yourself a long enough time to get established before you go on to more expensive elements.

Printing

The least expensive - and most practical - way to print your newsletter is an instant printer, using photo offset. These small local businesses can print, collate, fold, and stuff into envelopes - all for a reasonable fee.

If you want to use two colors in the newsletter, first have your masthead and perhaps border designs printed in huge quantities. All the black type can later be printed on those two-color pre-printed sheets.

Don't go to the expense of elaborate printing until your subscription volume is high and you advance into a different format. Almost any publication you read - newspapers, books, magazines-are printed on large roll presses and require typesetting.

Typesetting is expensive, but it certainly gives a professional finish to publications. Consider, however, if you want your newsletter to be slick. It may detract from its personal approach, and subscribers may drop if it leans towards a magazine.

But, if your subscription list is large and the newsletter is successful, you can find excellent printers who will handle the whole job of typesetting, layout, and printing - all the way to mailing.

How Often To Publish

There are a lot of factors to consider when deciding upon a publication schedule. The main one is how fast can you produce a newsletter. Work backwards. You want a subscriber to receive the newsletter on a certain date. It needs to be in the mail a few days before that. And before that, it will take the printer how many days to deliver the printed materials. How long will it take a typist to finish the copy, and for you to decide on the final layout?

How long will it take you to research and write material for your newsletter? This may be a deciding factor in the size of the publication. Perhaps you'd prefer to get a four page newsletter out every other week rather than an eight-page newsletter out every month.

Getting Subscribers

Think about where the people who would want your newsletter are, and go find them. Do you have access to mailing lists directly related to your subject matter? Maybe you already know of a small business selling information, or have access to a customer list of people who buy similar information.

You can purchase mailing lists that have every demographic breakdown you can imagine. What is the profile of your potential subscribers? Think about those people, and write down their attributes. Write down the age group, sex, education level, income, where they live, perhaps the type of housing accommodation. A good list broker can work out the best lists to give you results. How high can you price your newsletter and still keep the number of subscribers to make it profitable?

Mailing

You'll find through testing that there's a plateau, and subscriptions will fall off when the price gets too high. You can use computer services in your town to have labels printed up, or, if you're only dealing in a small quantity, you can have mailing lists photocopied onto address labels. After your first success, after you've paid your initial investment and you've got enough money to expand, make things easy on yourself. The most sophisticated, and the easiest method of mailing to subscribers is by computer.

Nowadays, computers are so commercially popular that they are within almost anybody's budget. And a computer that would store and print out names and addresses need not be expensive. If the mail is pre-sorted by zip code, you can use a bulk rate for mailing and save money. If your newsletter meets the specifications, you might even be able to get a special second class rate permit for educational material. Talk with the postal workers to find out what you need to do to comply with these special rates.

What's Legal

Although any business in the United States is subject to the Federal Trade Commission's regulations, a newsletter business is simple. You don't need a license for this business. However, you should consult with your local Sales Tax office for acquiring a resale tax permit.

The content of the newsletter must be documented by facts if you get into any dispute. If you don't border on libel, you should have no problem with any law suits for the content of your publication. However, consult your attorney if there are any problems with copyright, confidentiality, or access to news. If you write with integrity, independent of any payoffs by companies or individuals, you'll have no trouble staying on the right side of the law.

Finally Success Is Yours

Writing and publishing a newsletter is a challenging and exciting way to express yourself. And it will give you prestige and acknowledgment in the community.

You can start the business with virtually no overhead, a small amount of capital, and you can build up to making profits in the six-figure bracket.

10 Common Marketing Mistakes to Avoid

- **Not marketing to a Defined Group:** Find your target audience and gear your marketing plan to that audience. Trying to appeal to everyone typically does not work.
- **Inconsistency in Your Marketing Efforts**: You need to have the same look and feel across all of your ads, promotions and overall marketing plan.
- **Lack of Diversification:** Marketing on television, in print or on the Internet alone will reach only a portion of your potential customers. Plan to market creatively through a cross-section of media so that customers become familiar with your brand and your products at different times and in different places.
- **Not Focusing on Repeat Business:** Repeat business typically makes up 80 percent of customers in most businesses. Too often marketing campaigns are heavily focused on bringing in new customers and not building relationships with current ones.
- **Starting Too Late:** Time your marketing campaigns to coincide with new products, new services, seasonal sales or an upcoming event that will attract business. This typically means preparing well in advance.
- **Not Having a Clear Marketing Message:** Marketing messages that are contrived, confusing, too subtle or too long can easily miss the target market entirely. The most ingenious marketing plan is wasted if no one gets it.
- **Going Overboard:** If it sounds too good to be true it probably is. Too much hype will turn people away.
- **Forgetting That Slow and Steady Wins the Race:** If you blow your entire marketing budget on a Super Bowl ad, then what can you do next? Marketing means building a reputation over time through ongoing exposure.
- **Not Getting Feedback:** Test your marketing ideas and do focus groups. Don't launch it without getting some feedback first.

- **Making a Change for the Sake of It:** Just because you are tired of your marketing plan doesn't mean it isn't working. Too many marketers make changes because they think they have too. Often a tried and true formula will keep working

12 Most Common Direct Mail Mistakes

...And How to Avoid Them

Mistake No. 1: Ignoring the most important factor in direct mail success.

Do you know what the most important part of your direct mail campaign is? It's not the copy. It's not the art work. It's not even the format or when you mail. It is the mailing list.

A great mailing package, with superior copy and great design, might pull double the response of a poorly conceived mailing. But the best list can pull a response 10 times more than the worst list for the identical mailing piece.

The most common direct-mail mistake is not spending enough time and effort up-front. Remember: In direct marketing, a mailing list is not just a way of reaching your market. It is the market.

The best list available to you is your "house" list - a list of customers and prospects that previously bought from you or responded to your ads, public relations campaign, or other mailings. Typically, your house list will pull double the response of an outside list. Yet, only 50% of business marketers, I've surveyed, capture and use customer and prospect names for mailing purposes.

When renting outside lists, get your ad agency or list broker involved in the early stages. The mailing piece should not be written and designed until after the right lists have been identified and selected.

Mistake No. 2: Not testing.

Big consumer mailers test all the time. Publishers Clearinghouse tests just about everything...even (I hear) the slant of the font on the outer envelope.

Business-to-business marketers, on the other hand, seldom track response or test one mailing piece of list against another. As a result, they repeat their failures and have no idea of what works in direct mail - and what doesn't. This is a mistake. In direct mail, you should not assume you know what will work. You should test to find out.

For example, copywriter Milt Pierce wrote a subscription package for Good Housekeeping magazine. His mailing became the "control" package for 25 years. That is, no package tested against it brought back as many subscriptions.

The envelope teaser and theme of that successful mailing was "32 Ways to Save Time and Money." Yet, Mr. Pierce says that when he applied the same theme to subscription mailings for other magazines - Science Digest, Popular Mechanics, and House Beautiful - it failed miserably.

"There are no answers in direct mail except test answers," says Eugene Schwartz, author of the book, "Break-through advertising." "You don't know whether something will work until you test it. And you cannot predict test results based on past experience."

Mistake No. 3: Not using a letter in your mailing package.

The sales letter, the brochure, or even the reply form - is the most important part of your direct-mail package, not the outer envelope.

A package with a letter will nearly always outdo a postcard, a self-mailer, or a brochure or ad reprint mailed without a letter.

Recently, a company tested two packages offering, for $1, a copy of its mail-order tool catalog. Package "A" consisted of a sales letter and reply form. Package "B" was a double post-card. The result? "A" outdid "B" by a 3-to-1 ratio.

Why do letters do so well? Because a letter creates the illusion of personal communication. We are trained to view letters as "real" mail, brochures as "advertising." Which is more important to you? One recommendation I often give clients is to try an old-fashioned sales letter first. Go to a fancier package once you start making some money.

Mistake No. 4: Features vs. Benefits.

Perhaps the oldest and most widely embraced rule for writing direct-mail copy is, "Stress benefits, not features." But in business-to-business marketing, that doesn't always hold true.

In certain situations, features must be given equal (if not top) billing over benefits.

For example, if you've ever advertised semiconductors, you know that design engineers are hungry for specs. They want hard data on drain-source, voltage, power dissipation, input capacitance, and rise-and-fall time...not broad advertising claims about how the product helps save time and money or improves performance. "I've tested many mailings selling engineering components and products to OEMs (original equipment manufacturers)," says Don Jay Smith, president of the Chatham, NJ-based ad agency The Wordsmith. "I've found that features and specs out pull benefits almost every time."

Vivian Sudhalter, Director of Marketing for New York-based Macmillan Software Co., agrees. "Despite what tradition tells you," says Ms. Sudhalter, "the engineering and scientific marketplace does not respond to promise - or benefit - oriented copy. They respond to features. Your copy must tell them exactly what they are getting and what your product can do. Scientists and engineers are put off by copy that sounds like advertising jargon."

In the same way, I suspect that doctors are swayed more by hard medical data than by advertising claims, and that industrial chemists are eager to learn about complex formulations that the average advertising writer might reject as "too technical."

In short, the copywriter's real challenge is to find out what the customer wants to know about your product - and then tell him in your mailing.

Mistake No. 5: Not having an offer.

An offer is what the reader gets when he responds to your mailing. To be successful, a direct-mail package should sell the offer, not the product itself.

For example, if I mail a letter describing a new model computer, my letter is not going to do the whole job of convincing people to buy my computer. But the letter is capable of swaying some people to at least show interest by requesting a free brochure about the computer. Make sure you have a well-thought-out offer in every mailing. If you think the offer and the way you describe it are unimportant, you are wrong.

A free-lance copywriter friend of mine ran an ad in the Wall Street Journal that offered a free portfolio of article reprints about direct mail. He received dozens of replies. Then he ran an identical ad, but charged $3 for the portfolio instead of giving it away. Number of responses that time were only three.

Here are some effective offers for industrial direct mail: Free brochure, free technical information, free analysis, free consultation, free demonstration, free trial use, free product sample, free catalog. Your copy should state the offer in such a way as to increase the reader's desire to send for whatever it is you offer. For example, a catalog becomes a product guide. A collection of brochures becomes a free information kit. A checklist becomes a convention planner's guide. An article reprinted in pamphlet form becomes "our new, informative booklet-'How to Prevent Computer Failures.'"

From now on, design your fulfillment literature with titles and information that will make them work well as offers in direct mail. When one of my clients decided to publish a catalog listing US software programs available for export overseas, I persuaded her to call the book "The international Directory of US Software," because I thought people would think such a directory was more valuable than a mere product catalog.

Mistake No. 6: Superficial copy.

Nothing kills the selling power of a business-to-business mailing faster than lack of content.

The equivalent in industrial literature is what I call the "art director's brochure." You've seen them: Showcase pieces destined to win awards for graphic excellence. Brochures so gorgeous that everybody falls in love with them - until they wake up and realize that people send for information, not pretty pictures. Which is why typewritten, un-illustrated sales brochures can often pull double the response of expensive, four-color work.

In the same way, direct mail is not meant to be pretty. Its goal is not to be remembered or create an image or make an impact, but to generate a response now. One of the quickest ways to kill that response is to be superficial; to talk in vague generalities, rather than specifics. To ramble without authority on a subject, rather than show customers that you understand their problems, their industries and their needs.

What causes superficial copy? The fault lies with lazy copywriters who don't bother to do their homework (or ignorant copywriters who don't know any better).

To write strong copy - specific, factual copy - you must dig for facts. You must study the product, the prospect and the marketing problem. There is no way around this. Without facts, you cannot write good copy. But with the facts at their fingertips, even mediocre copywriters can do a decent job.

Don Hauptman, author of the famous mail-order ad, “Speak Spanish Like a Diplomat!” says that when he writes a direct-mail package, more than 50% of the work involved is in the reading, research and preparation. Less than half his time is spent writing, rewriting, editing and revising.

Recently a client hired me to write an ad on a software package. After reading the background material and typing it into my word processor, I had 19 single-spaced pages of notes.

How much research is enough? Follow Bly’s Rule, which says you should collect at least twice as much information as you need - preferably three times as much. Then you have the luxury of selecting only the best facts, instead of trying desperately to find enough information to fill up the page.

Mistake No. 7: Saving the best for last.

Some copywriters save their strongest sales pitch for last, starting slow in their sales letters and hoping to build to a climactic conclusion.

Leo Bott, Jr., a Chicago-based mail-order writer, says that “ the typical prospect reads for five seconds before he decides whether to continues reading or throw your mailing in the trash.” The letter must grab his attention immediately. So start your letter with your strongest sales point. Some examples of powerful openings:

“14 things that can go wrong in your company - and one sure way to prevent them” - an envelope teaser for a mailing that sold a manual on internal auditing procedures.

“A special invitation to the hero of American business” - from a subscription letter for Inc. magazine.

“Can 193,750 millionaires be wrong?” - An envelope teaser for a subscription mailing for Financial World magazine.

“Dear Friend: I’m fed up with the legal system. I want to change it, and I think you do, too.” - The lead paragraph of a fund-raising letter. Some time-testing opening gambits for sales letters include:

Asking a provocative question:

- going straight to the heart of the reader’s most pressing problem or concern
- arousing curiosity; leading off with a fascinating fact or incredible statistic

- Starting the offer up-front, especially if it involves money, saving it, getting something for an incredibly low price
- or making a free offer.

Know the "hot spots" of your direct mail package - the paces that get the most readerships. Those include: the first paragraphs of the letter, its subheads, its last paragraph and the post-script (80% of readers look at the PS); the brochure cover, its subheads and the headline of its inside spread; picture captions; and the headline and copy on the order form or reply card. Put your strongest selling copy in those spots.

Mistake No. 8: Poor follow-up.

Recently a company phoned to ask whether I was interested in buying its product, which was promoted in a mailing I'd answered. The caller became indignant when I confessed that I didn't remember the company's copy, its product, its mailing, or whether it sent me a brochure.

"When did I request the brochure?" I asked. The caller checked her records. "About 14 weeks ago," she replied. Hot leads rapidly turn ice cold when not followed up quickly. Slow fulfillment, poor marketing literature, and inept telemarketing can destroy the initial interest that you worked so hard to build.

Here are some questions you should ask yourself about your current inquiry fulfillment procedures:

Am I filling orders or requests for information within 48 hours?

- Am I using telephone follow-up or mail questionnaires to qualify prospects? By definition, an inquiry is a response to your mailing. A lead is a qualified inquirer - someone who fits the descriptive profile of a potential customer for your product. You are after leads, not just inquiries.
- Am I sending additional mailings to people who did not respond to my first mailing? Test that. Many people who did not respond to mailing No. 1 may send back the reply card from mailing No. 2, or even No. 3.
- Am I using telemarketing to turn non-responders into responders? Direct mail followed by telemarketing generates two to 10 times more response than direct mail with no telephone follow-up, according to Dwight Reichard, telemarketing director of Federated Investors Inc., Pittsburgh.

- Does my inquiry fulfillment package include a strong sales letter telling the prospect what to do next? Every package should include this.
- Does my inquiry fulfillment package include a reply element, such as an order form or spec sheet?
- Does my sales brochure give the reader the information he needs to make an intelligent decision about taking the next step in the buying process? The most common complaints I hear from prospects is that the brochures they receive do not contain enough technical and price information.
- Don't put 100% of your time and effort into lead-generating mailing and 0% into the follow-up, as so many salespersons do. You have to keep selling, every step of the way.

Mistake No. 9: The magic words.

What are the magic words of direct mail that can dramatically increase the response to your mailing. General advertisers, operating under the mistaken notion that the mission of the copywriter is to be creative, avoid magic words of direct mail, because they think these magic phrases are clichés. But just because a word or phrase is used frequently doesn't mean that it has lost its power to achieve your communications objective. In conversation, for example, "please" and "thank you" never go out of style.

What are the magic words of direct mail?

Free. Say free brochure. Not brochure. Say free consultation. Not initial consultation. Say free gift. Not gift. If the English teacher in you objects that "free gift" is redundant, let me tell you a story. A mail-order firm tested two packages. The only difference was that package "A" offered a gift while package "B" offered a free gift. The result? You guessed it. The free gift order in package "B" significantly out pulled package "A". What's more, many people who received package "A" wrote in and asked whether the gift was free!

No Obligation. This is important when you are offering anything free. If prospects aren't obligated to use your firm's wastewater treatment services after you analyze their water sample for free, say so. People want to be reassured that there are no strings attached.

Details inside/See inside. One of these should follow any teaser copy on the outer envelope. You need a phrase that directs the reader to the inside.

Limited time only. People who put your mailing aside for later reading or file it will probably never respond. The trick is to generate a response now. One way to do it is with a time-limited offer, either generic ("This offer is for a limited time only."), or specific ("This offer expires 9/20/87."). Try it!

Announcing/At last. People like to think they are getting in on the ground floor of a new thing. Making your mailing an announcement increases its attention-getting powers.

New. "New" is sheer magic in consumer mailings. But it's a double-edged sword in industrial mailings. On the one hand, business and technical buyers want something new. On the other hand, they demand products with proven performance.

The solution? Explain that your product is new or available to them for the first time, but proven elsewhere - either in another country, another application, or another industry. For example, when we introduced a diagnostic display system, we advertised it as "new" to US hospitals but explained it had been used successfully for five years in leading hospitals throughout the United States.

Mistake No. 10: Starting with the product - not the prospect.

You and your products are not important to the prospect. The reader opening your sales letter only wants to know, "What's in it for me? How will I come out ahead by doing business with you vs. someone else?"

Successful direct mail focuses on the prospect, not the product. The most useful background research you can do is to ask your typical prospect, "What's the biggest problem you have right now?" The sales letter should talk about that problem, and then promise a solution.

Do not guess what is going on in industries about which you have limited knowledge. Instead, talk to customers and prospects to find out their needs. Read the same publications and attend the same seminars they do. Try to learn their problems and concerns.

Too many companies and ad agencies don't do this. Too many copywriters operate in a black box, and doom themselves merely to recycling data already found in existing brochures. For example, let's say you have the assignment of writing a direct-mail package selling weed control chemicals to farmers. Do you know what farmers look for in weed control, or why they choose one supplier over another? Unless you are a farmer, you probably don't. Wouldn't it be helpful to speak to some farmers and learn more about their situation? Read, talk and listen to find out what's going on with your customers.

In his book "Or Your Money Back," Alvin Eicoff, one of the deans of late night television commercials, tells the story of a radio commercial he wrote selling rat poison. It worked well in the consumer market. But when it was aimed at the farm market, sales turned up zero. Mr. Eicoff drove out to the country to talk with farmers. His finding? Farmers didn't order because they were embarrassed about having a rat problem, and feared their neighbors would learn about it when the poison was delivered by mail.

He added a single sentence to the radio script, which said that the rat poison was mailed in a plain brown wrapper. After that, sales soared. Talk to your customers. Good direct mail--or any ad copy--should tell them what they want to hear. Not what you think is important.

Mistake No. 11: Failing to appeal to all five senses.

Unlike an ad, which is two-dimensional, direct mail is three-dimensional and can appeal to all five senses: sight, hearing, touch, smell, taste. Yet most users of direct mail fail to take advantage of the medium's added dimension. Don't plan a mailing without at least thinking about whether you can make it more powerful by adding a solid object, fragrance or even a sound. You ultimately may reject such enhancements because of time and budget constraints. But here are some ideas you might consider:

CD. In selling summaries of business books recorded on cassette, Macmillan Software Co. sent a CD in a cold mailing to prospects. The cassette allows the prospect to sample the books-on-CD program. I would have said, "Too expensive." But inside information, and the fact that I got the package twice, tell me it's working for them. Do you have a powerful message that a company spokesperson can deliver in dynamic fashion to your audience? Consider adding a CD to your package.

DVD's. Some companies are taking the idea one step further and mailing DVD's cold to prospects. Again, that's expensive--but successful in many instances. One company I spoke to got a 30% response to such a program. And in telephone follow-up, they learned that 95% watched the DVD.

Pop-ups. Chris Crowell, president of Essex, Conn.-based Structural Graphics Inc., says pop-ups can increase response up to 40% when compared with a conventional flat mailing. You can have a pop-up custom designed for your mailing or choose from one of many "stock" designs available.

Money. Market research firms have discovered that enclosing a two dollar bill with a market research survey can increase response by a factor of five or more, even though $2 is surely of no consequence to business executives or most consumers.

Sound. Have you seen the greeting cards that play a song when you open them because of an implanted chip or some similar device? I think that certainly would get attention. But as far as I know, no one has used it yet in direct mail.

Product samples. Don't neglect this old standard. Enclose a product or material sample in your next mailing. We once did a mailing in which we enclosed a small sample of knitted wire mesh used in pollution control and product recovery. Engineers who received the mailing kept that bit of wire on their desks for months.

Premiums. An inexpensive gift such as a slide guide, measuring tape, ruler or thermometer can still work well.

Mistake No. 12: Creating and reviewing direct mail by committee.

Do you know what a moose is? It's a cow designed by a committee. Perhaps the biggest problem I see today is direct mail being reviewed by committees made up of people who have no idea (a) what direct mail is; (b) how it works; or (c) what it can and cannot do.

For example, an ad agency creative director told me how his client cut a three-page sales letter to a single page because, as the client insisted, "Business people don't read long letters."

Unfortunately, that's an assumption based on the client's own personal prejudices and reading habits. It is not a fact. In many business-to-business direct mail tests, I have seen long letters out pull short ones sometimes dramatically.

Why pay experts to create mailings based on long years of trial-and-error experience, and then deprive yourself of that knowledge base by letting personal opinions get in the way?

Here are some things you can do to become a better direct-mail client:

Reduce the review process. The fewer people who are involved, the better. At most, the mailing should be checked by the communications manager, the product manager and a technical expert (for accuracy).

Resist the temptation to meddle. Point out technical inaccuracies and other mistakes. But don't dictate the piece's content, tone or style. Make a commitment to judge direct mail not by what you like or by aesthetics, but by results-which can be measured accurately and scientifically. Become more educated in direct mail by reading books. Know what's going on in the industry. Subscribe to at least one of the direct marketing magazines: Direct Marketing, Zip Target Marketing, and DM Nexus. Also, keep in touch with industry developments by reading the more broadly based marketing publications, such as Business Marketing and Advertising Age. If you challenge your direct mail pros, be willing to spend for a test. In direct mail, the answer to "Which concept is best?" is the same as the answer to the question, "Which mailing piece pulled best?"

CHAPTER 7
INTERNET MARKETING

"In the coming decade marketing will be reengineered from A to Z. There is little doubt that markets and marketing will operate on quite different principles in the early years of the twenty-first century. The successor of the Industrial Society - the Information Economy - will penetrate and change almost every aspect of daily life. The Digital Revolution has fundamentally altered concepts of space, time, and mass. A company need not occupy much space: it can be virtual and anywhere. Messages can be sent and received simultaneously. And such objects as books, music, and film can be shipped in the forms of "bits" rather than mass.

Today there are more than 300 million people worldwide who can connect to the Internet. More than 2 million domain names are registered on the Internet. Traffic is estimated to double every hundred days. E-commerce was $20 billion in 1998 and is expected to rise to $700 billion by A.D. 2009

Cyberspace will usher in an age when buying and selling will become more automated and convenient. Businesses will be connected to each other and to their customers in a seamless virtual network. Information on the Internet will flow across the globe in an instant and at no cost. Sellers will find it easier to identify potential buyers; and buyers will find it easier to identify the best sellers and products. Time and distance, which acted, as great cost and trade barriers in the past, will shrink immeasurable. Merchants who continue to sell in the old ways will slowly vanish from the scene.

Marketers will need to rethink fundamentally the process by which they identify, communicate, and deliver customer value. They will need to improve their skills in managing individual customers and allies. They will need to involve their customers in the act of code signing their desired products."

Kotler on Marketing

PPC or CPC

What is PPC (Pay per Click) or CPC (Cost per Click) search engine placement?

These are sponsored listings. Web sites must pay for placement in the search engines. Fee structure of these services range from flat rate to bidding against your competitors for your selected keywords. For example, to be a sponsored listing with Google you must go directly to Google and open an account and agree to pay a fee for every time your link is clicked on. Once this is done, your site will appear along the right hand side of the natural listings in colored boxes under the title "sponsored links".

SEO

What is SEO (Search Engine Optimization?)

It is the act of modifying or creating the opportunity for a website to make the best possible argument on its behalf as to why it is most relevant to a selected keyword or key-phrase according to the search engine algorithms.

What is the difference between SEO and PPC or CPC?

SEO will get your site listed in the natural section of a search engine. This section displays its results and rankings based on which site is most relevant to the searched word. PPC or CPC results are based upon paying clients of the engine. SEO is a long term strategy. SEO is by far the most cost effective way of getting search engine placement. PPC lasts as long as your account has funds.

What is the difference between SEO and SEM (Search Engine Marketing)?

The goal of an SEO company is to get you ranked. The goal of an SEM (Search Engine Marketing) company is to get you clients. SEM companies focus on getting you ranked with enticing descriptions while SEO's don't care. SEM's focuses on your site as a whole, not just a page on top of the engines. SEM's don't just want to deliver traffic, they also want conversions to sales.

Guaranteed #1 ranking in 48 hours and how you can do this yourself for free.

When companies give guarantees such as these, be careful of the fine print. No one can guarantee top placement in the natural search results in 48 or even 72 hours except the engines themselves. Don't believe the hype. However, anyone can open a PPC account with Overture and get themselves placed in the #1 position of Yahoo (in the sponsored section) without having to pay a third party broker extra fees. Don't fall for this; you can do this on your own.

Some Guidelines to Follow

1. **NEVER** (I mean Never, Ever, Never) sign up with a web hosting company that does not offer 24 hour, 7 day a week support. That means live support, not automated replies. If you do not have the ability to speak with a live person via telephone or email, you will sooner or later will be in dire straits. Test the support *before* signing up with the web host.

2. **Do NOT** sign up with a web host without first contacting a handful of their current customers and asking them about support. (Not referrals that they give you, but customers that you find. You can do this by visiting their bulletin board area or chat room, if they have one. If not, ask them for a long list of customers you can contact and call lots of them.)

3. **Do NOT** let your domain be registered under someone else's name. Make sure YOU are the administrative contact. This will allow you to transfer your domain without your host being involved. It will

speed things up and give you the freedom that you're rightfully deserved.

4. **Put two items high on your list**: Peering and Mirroring. Peering is having multiple backbones coordinated in such a way that when one line gets too slow the server is automatically switched to the fastest line out. While many providers have "multiple connections" to the Internet a very, few percentage of them are able to truly "peer". This means your site will always be connected at the fastest speed available. Similarly, "mirroring" means placing servers at different locations. This not only serves as a back-up, but it enhances your site's accessibility and connection speeds from all over the world.

5. **ALWAYS keep YOUR OWN back-up copy of your site**. As a matter of fact, keep fresh copies on your hard drive and weekly or monthly copies on a zip disk or tape backup. Never rely on your web hosting company's promise of back-up. If you are considering putting a web site up, make sure you follow the guidelines above. If you already have a web site, take a hard look at your current web host. Is it a disaster waiting to happen?

6. **Send a message to your support team** and see how long it takes them to get back to you. If you are even a little concerned, you may have good reason to be. If so, don't wait until you're counting your losses. If you have ever considered moving your site to a more responsive, professional host, take it from me - it's much easier to act than react. Once the nightmare starts, cyberspace is a cold and lonely place.

Motivating Your Web Site Visitors

This section is based on a variation of the Myers-Briggs Type Indicator and Kiersey Temperament Sorters. The idea behind personality targeting is that people are generally motivated to different degrees by the following four qualities:

- Power / Status
- Competition / Cutting Edge

- Connectedness / Community
- Money / Price

So how do you decide which type to target? Well, you can either pick one type and go after those customers or try to cover all the bases in some way with your site. It's easier than you think.

Here's a rundown on the different personality types and some ideas on how to appeal to your specific audience.

Power / Status:

People who fall into this category want to be seen as important people. They look for products and services that reinforce that image. Targeting this group is great if you're selling high-value items. Try to position your product/service/message as an important, prestigious thing. Celebrity endorsements are given a lot of weight with this crowd. These people generally have newer computer equipment and run the latest operating system versions, so you have a little more leeway when using different technologies in your site design such as JavaScript and DHTML.

A website designed to appeal to the power/status segment should be very professional, and the copywriting should convey a tone of exclusiveness. Prices may not be published; after all, if you have to ask...! Examples would be high-end automobiles, wedding photographers, fundraising balls.

Competition / Cutting Edge

People in this group are fashion-forward dressers, video-gamers and technology enthusiasts. They seek challenge and creativity. High-ticket items are no problem for this crowd since they are willing to pay a premium to get what they want before the rest of the market. A sales message to these people should emphasize the latest, greatest, fastest and the most unique features of the offering.

This group also has newer equipment and the latest browser. Your website design might feature more "bells and whistles" such as flash animation, DHTML/JavaScript mouseovers, demos and movies. Colors and design may be slightly unsettling and cutting edge -- meant to be noticed. Customization, personalization and "skins" appeal to these customers. Examples of companies who would target this group would be electronics sites, website designers, art galleries, etc.

Connectedness / Community:

Those that fall into this group are the caretakers of the world. They worry about the environment, community issues, friends and family. They like familiar, accepted things. They are likely to wait until an item becomes a commodity that is in wide use before adopting it. Their browser and equipment are probably older, but still functional. A website catering to this crowd should emphasize content and advice and have simple navigation with a logical layout. The more information, the better. A comforting, simple color scheme is also important.

Recognition of events that affect our lives (e.g., 9-11, the Space Shuttle disaster) is appropriate and appreciated by this group. High-value items can be sold to this group if they are positioned correctly. They are glad to pay more for items that are environmentally-friendly or family-friendly. This group likes it when you remember who they are the next time they visit, so website personalization can be helpful when targeting them. Some companies who would target this group might be "Made in the USA" products, Internet picture frame companies, chambers of commerce, etc.

Money / Price:

There are plenty of people in the world who shop by price alone, and for them you need to offer specials and discounts. Make it easy for them to buy so they don't wander off and find your products/services cheaper elsewhere. These people need to be grabbed and called to action when they first visit your site.

For the price-conscious, limited-time offers are a good motivator. A site design for them should make it easy for them to find what they're looking for, along with good information and prices. Be sure to include a site-search function and create the site so that it loads quickly and without gimmicks. Things like pop-up windows or slow-loading animations irritate this group and will make them leave. A huge plus for this group is a feature comparison chart. They also appreciate signing up for a newsletter that will notify them when items are on sale.

A fancy design could put this crowd off because they don't want to pay for *your* marketing. Bright, active colors work well. Examples of the type of sites that might target these people are software companies, printer ink sales, cell phones, etc.

It is easy to focus on one personality type with your design, layout and copy, but with a little creativity you can actually build a site that appeal to all four types.

When outlining the content for any given page of your site, try writing a heading and a paragraph that would appeal to each type. Better yet, try linking to a page where you can write copy that specifically speaks to that particular personality type. This way, those interested can click to the exact information they're looking for!

Vertical Search Lines

Vertical search refers to search engines designed to return results from very narrow or specific information or business sectors. Search tools that focus on a tight regime of information have existed for years. There are plenty of examples that already exist such as the highly successful book-search engine, AbeBooks.com, or the various job and career search engines like Monster.com. Name a business sector and you can likely find a search tool designed specifically for that sector.

Look Smart Looking Before Leaping

Seeing the growing interest in Vertical Search, LookSmart has introduced five new vertical search engines, each of which draws from LookSmart's database. Focusing on teens, students, families and women, these vertical search features are a way for LookSmart to test the waters of this market without actually reinventing its brand. For teens and college students, Teenja.com, GradeWinner.com and 24hourscholar.

com provide information and entertainment options targeted at three distinct youth markets. Parents can find information on child raising, nutrition and entertainment options for families at ParentSurf while the busy mother-on-the-go can find information for time-stressed moms at Go Belle.

These five vertical search engines will soon be available on one page via LookSmart's web-community Furl. After the user finds information using one of the five new vertical search tools, Furl users can save content to a personal archive and easily share that information with others. Furl is also a social network with topical archives built on recommendations from its members.

"LookSmart believes that search on the Web will become increasingly vertical and personal. Consumers turn to the Web in search of essential content as it is related to a hobby, work or education," said Debby Richman, senior vice president of consumer products for LookSmart in a recent press release. "The new verticals were developed to build upon LookSmart's core demographics of researchers and families from the company's existing consumer products, Find Articles and Net Nanny."

Why Vertical Search is Important

Traditionally, search engines are thought of to be general information resources from which a wide range of information can be extracted based on general keywords. As the Internet becomes more populated with both users and content, a migration from general information sources to specific information sources is natural. Trying to find a used car of any type using Goggle's general search engine is like trying to find a grain of sand in a glass vase. A search engine dedicated to used cars on the other hand would likely guide the user to more accurate information faster than a general search tool would.

This sort of thinking makes a lot of sense when you stop to think about it. Why should I arrange my travel plans, (a major investment of a critical two week period in an otherwise work-a-day year), using a general, commercialized search engine when faster and more specific alternatives are emerging? It seems rather like buying an off the rack suit when a tailored one is available for a similar cost. This might be a mistake however. While the major search engines (Goggle, Yahoo, MSN and Ask Jives) are considered by many to be "general search engines", each of them offers some form of vertical search features.

Local search, a feature offered by nearly every major search engine is considered a variant on the concept of Vertical Search. By narrowing the field of results to a relatively small geographic area, local-search features offered by the major search engines make a mountain of information into a well-mapped molehill.

Each of the majors offers some form of localized search, and each is expanding ways to help users narrow their search results to find information as quickly as possible.

As a measure of how seriously the major search tools are taking "vertical search", Goggle recently listed seven management level jobs in its emerging Vertical Search division.

Search engine users should expect to see a wave of sector-specific search tools emerge in the coming months. A lot of money is being pumped into smaller companies and start-ups to create search engines for unique companies or business sectors. The big search engines, which already offer vertical channels under different names, will start to re-brand those various channels as Vertical Search tools.

Businesses and search engine marketers should watch emerging search tools and the established search engines to see if they or their clients can benefit from the growth of this sub-sector of search. There is nothing wrong with more consumer options and an expansion of the marketing tools offered by the Internet. Ultimately, it will be the users who determine if Vertical Search tools are viable as businesses. If they are, great interest will continue to rise. If they are not however, Newtonian rules will apply. Any object that goes up in a vertical line will come down in a similar vertical line.

The Myth of Rankings

What follows is a condensed version of a conversation that happens all too frequently when businesses are interested in search engine optimization (SEO):

- Prospect: We need our website optimized, because we aren't showing up for any searches.
- Me: What searches have you tried?
- Prospect: We don't show up for anything.
- Me: Why do you want to show up in searches?
- Prospect: Well, it seems like we should. Our competitors do, and our website is WAY better than theirs.
- Me: But, really, what would you stand to gain from showing up prominently in search engine results?
- Prospect: Well, we could get more people who are looking for our products or services to find out about us.
- Me: So, what you are saying is that increasing your search engine results could help you to increase sales and awareness?
- Prospect: Yes.
- Me: Now we're on the right track. Since your goals are to increase sales and awareness, have you thought about doing more than just improving your search engine rankings, but also getting more people to take an action on your site that leads to a sale, getting more people to read your press releases or whitepapers so that they can consistently associate your company with your offering, or sending your prospects a regular newsletter to reinforce your name and expertise?
- Prospect: Didn't you hear me? Our website is great. We just don't show up for searches.

And so it goes.

A consistent problem with the "ranking-centric" mindset demonstrated above is that it doesn't reflect a powerful rationale for getting involved in

SEO. Where is the true business case? What tangible results are desired? In general, if a prospect can't explain what he or she hopes to achieve beyond "higher rankings" or "more traffic," we'll first try to educate, and, if that person can't move beyond these base subjects, we'll kindly refer them elsewhere.

More and more frequently, people are getting into SEO for the wrong reasons (and sometimes for no real reason at all). Achieving high rankings for targeted key phrases, while an admirable and worthwhile goal, is really only a small piece of the entire online marketing puzzle.

Website Conversion

Website conversion is the art and science of getting more of the people who come to your website to take the action that you want them to take – fill out your contact form, read your whitepapers, sign up for your newsletter, or (in the case of e-commerce) buy something. For a company that is trying to build offline business, this action is typically something that gets prospects into the sales pipeline through some form of online registration. For a company or organization that is trying to build awareness, this action can be a number of things – getting visitors to a certain page of the site, getting them to stay longer at the site, or getting them to tell a friend about the site.

The critical point that is commonly overlooked in a ranking-centric mindset is that no number of high search engine positions will address the real problem if your website is not serving as an effective marketing and sales tool. And, as I have said many times before, the overall net effect of raising your conversion rate from one to two percent is the same net effect as doubling your traffic, and it is almost always easier. Increasing the number of visitors to a site that does not convert them effectively is like pumping high performance gasoline into a car with engine trouble – it might help the car to run a little bit better, but if you'd done repairs before adding the premium fuel, it really would have hummed.

Online PR

Your website is only one potential online destination where people can find out about your company, and a typical user will regard your site as an advertisement since you have complete control over the content. With optimized press releases and expert articles, however, you can have your company name mentioned on popular news sites and industry portals, where credibility is more inherent.

Optimized Press Releases

Press releases that are optimized to appear when certain terms are typed into news search engines are an excellent way to build name recognition and credibility. If someone is taking the time to look for news related to your industry, he or she is probably either in your business, learning about your market, or writing a piece about your industry.

The last category is especially significant since a recent study* indicates that 98% of journalists go online daily, 92% use the Internet for article research, and 73% use it to find press releases. Whatever motivation a person has when he or she searches for news related to your industry, you want your company represented in the results.

Expert Articles

Another great way to promote your expertise and business is to write expert articles and submit them to the leading online publications in your field. At least one person in your company is almost certainly an expert in your field – why not let everyone know that? A person that reads an expert article published on an industry portal, and who subsequently clicks through to the website (from the link in the expert's bio) is extremely targeted and already has a favorable impression of your company.

Moreover, the same study cited above found that 76% of journalists go online to seek news sources or experts. When your company has demonstrated that you have experts on staff by publishing articles in credible, non-biased forums, the phone invariably starts to ring. Your experts will be asked to provide their opinions, quotes, or experiences for feature articles, often in prestigious industry publications. The benefits of this, of course, do not need explanation.

A side benefit to both of the strategies above is that they increase the number of inbound links to your website and, therefore, can help greatly enhance your search engine rankings – which might be the primary reason you looked into SEO in the first place.

Newsletters

Direct mail was once considered a marketer's dream – but email newsletters can be much more effective. Imagine a direct mail list with a low delivery cost, where every single person on the list has shown an interest in receiving such mailings. Such is the nature of opt-in email newsletters. People have shown enough interest in your company, or, at least, in what your company has to say, to invite you to communicate with them on a regular basis.

They are essentially giving you permission to keep yourself "first in mind" whenever they are considering your products or services. Such opportunities are rare in the marketing world. By combining the conversion principles you have applied to your website to your email newsletters, you can also get people to take an action that puts them into your sales pipeline without worrying about getting them to your website itself.

Conclusion

These are only a few of the additional ways to expand an online initiative beyond a misdirected ranking-centric approach. Blogs are often considered another new frontier in online marketing, and we haven't even touched on paid media opportunities such as banner ads or pay-per-click marketing. However, the three components mentioned above are important elements of a complete and successful online marketing initiative. An SEO campaign launched without considering them is like driving a four-cylinder car with only one cylinder firing – it will move, but you'd definitely reach your destination more quickly – and more smoothly – with all four.

Tips For Web Site Marketing Plans

For many of us, finding the time and commitment to develop an online marketing strategy is difficult. There are so many other obligations vying for our attention that it is tempting to push strategies to the back burner. Giving into that temptation, however, means putting your business at a disadvantage.

This is because an overall marketing strategy is the compass by which you navigate. As opportunities arise or your business environment changes, the objective and marketing strategies in your plan will point you toward the best action. Without a strategic plan, you risk becoming unfocused in your marketing efforts, resulting in guesses about what might be best for your business.

To be most effective, your Website (as well as other) marketing strategies should be a part of your overall business marketing plan. By aligning online marketing with your offline efforts, you can better achieve overall company objectives. Additionally, you will present a consistent style and message across all points of contact with your target audience

Your strategic focus will in part be determined by your site's status. If you already have a site in place, your plan can focus strictly on marketing issues. In other words, how to most effectively market using your existing site.

If you have a site that needs improvement, however, your marketing efforts will be more effective if you incorporate Website enhancements in with your strategies.

Finally, if you do not yet have a site, you can create one as you develop a marketing strategy, with your plan focused on launching the site. In any case, remember that your objective, strategies, and tactics will change over time as your situation and focus change.

Parts of a Marketing Plan

A strategic Website marketing plan is similar to a strategic business marketing plan, but with a narrower focus (i.e. the Website plan focuses on Internet marketing strategy and programs while the overall marketing plan encompasses the entire business).

As with any marketing plan, the online plan includes developing strategies and tactics (also called action plans) that, when implemented, will help you reach your marketing goals. An objective, strategy, and tactic are each progressively narrower in scope:

The objective addresses the "big picture". In general terms, your objective answers the question "How will I overcome my main marketing challenge(s)?" If your company's main site-related challenge is figuring out how to use your Website to help build client business, for example, an objective for your online marketing plan could be "To enhance online client service as well as build site awareness and interest with clients."

A marketing strategy supports your objective. The strategy defines general approaches you will take to meet your objective. For example, strategies to support the above objective could include

- Improve online communication, information, and education
- Build awareness of an interest in your company on the Internet
- Communicate the Website's existence and advantages to existing clients

A marketing tactic is where the action takes place

Also called marketing programs or action plans, they are the things you will do to bring each marketing strategy to life. Tactics for strategy 2 in the above example (improve online communication, information, and education) could include:

- sharing experience and observations in your industry through participation in discussion boards
- offering an email newsletter
- Listing/submitting your site to targeted search engines and directories

By implementing marketing programs that are consistent with your site objective(s) and marketing strategies you improve your chance of business success.

Your plan write-up should begin with a summary. The traditional "executive summary" is one option. I prefer to include - either in addition to or instead of the executive summary - a one-page table. The table makes everyday use of your plan easier. In one glance you can be reminded of your main challenge, objective, strategies, and tactics as well as budgets and deadlines. Also, as your plan evolves throughout the year, the table makes it easier to strategically modify the plan.

Explain your reasoning. Make some reference to why you chose the specific objective(s) and strategies in your plan. This will make it easier to justify the plan to others (if necessary). It will also help you make smarter, strategic decisions. Identify your target customers. By doing so, you will be better able to develop effective advertising messages.

Write one or more positioning statements. In the statement(s), specify the customer needs you are fulfilling, benefits your products/services offer, and features that deliver those benefits.

Explain key issues and opportunities. These can best be identified through industry and/or competitive analyses. Include preliminary budgets and timelines for your action plans.

Expanded Content for Your Marketing Plan You can also expand your marketing plan write-up to include detailed analysis and arguments to substantiate your plan: Describe the strengths, weaknesses, opportunities, and threats your business and/or Website face (SWOT analysis).

Explain the online business environment. Who are your competitors' Web strategies? How do your customers use your site, competing sites, and the Internet in general? What potential substitutes are available? Include the trends in your industry and how they affect both online and offline activity. Show growth projections.

Detail the financial aspects. Include break even analysis for your site as well as for the tactics included in your plan. Discuss assumptions made when completing your financial analysis. Show how implementation of your plan will be profitable to your business.

Include a calendar of events that shows milestones in the coming weeks or months. You can be as detailed or top-line as needed with the final marketing plan write-up. In any case remember that your marketing plan is always a work in progress. It may be current, but it is never "done".

Webinar

Webinar is short for Web-based seminar. Webinar's are just like a conference room based seminar; however, participants view the presentation through their Web-browser and listen to the audio through their telephone. A key feature of a Webinar is its interactive elements -- the ability to give, receive and discuss information. Contrast with "Webcast", in which the data transmission is one way and does not allow interaction between the presenter and the audience.

What are Webinars used for?

Webinar's are primarily used to train a large number of people or build brand and generate sales leads. Additional uses are: corporate announcements focus groups, and press conferences. What are the benefits?

- Reach a larger audience
- Reduce cost
- Digitally record and allow future playback

What do I need to attend?

1. A computer
2. Internet access
3. A phone line for listening to the teleconference portion

CHAPTER 8
HOW TO MASTER PR

Developing a Public Relations Campaign

The term "Public Relations" is a staple among business owners who utilize this practice to communicate key attributes of their company to prospective customers. Newly launched firms to established corporations use various facets of public relations to grow their companies. Yet the term is often misunderstood.

Many confuse public relations as simply "publicity". Others consider it a form of marketing. Some think of it as free advertising.

What Is Public Relations?

The concept of Public Relations is perhaps best defined by the book *Effective Public Relations(1)* which states...

Public Relations is the management function that identifies, establishes, and maintains mutually beneficial relationships between an organization and the various publics on whom its success or failure depends.

The Public Relations Society of America created the "Official Statement on Public Relations". Some of the highlights of this define the practice as...

- Anticipating, analyzing and interpreting public opinion, attitude and issues which might impact, for good or ill, the operations and plans of the organization.
- Researching, conducting and evaluating, on a continuing basis, programs of action and communication to achieve

informed public understanding necessary to the success of an organization's aims. These may include marketing, financial fund raising, employee, community or government relations and other programs.

- Planning and implementing the organization's efforts to influence or change public policy.

This author believes, for both new and established companies, one should look upon Public Relations as relationship building. The end result is creating new positive bonds between your firm and the customers you currently have or wish to serve.

What Public Relations Is Not

Public Relations is definitely not advertising, nor marketing in the purest sense, nor sales.

When a business places an ad in the local newspaper promoting a sale or new product it is *advertising*.

When a company discusses new product launches with regard to design, distribution channels, and procurement it is *marketing*.

When someone makes phone calls to secure appointments and visits various companies to sell a service or product it is obviously sales.

Many business owners make the mistake of believing that advertising is a form of public relations or that public relations is a form of advertising. So what's the difference between the two?

When a company purchases an advertisement they control the message. They select the size of the ad and the date, publication, and section it will run. The company also decides what the ad will say. It could be a sale, a grand opening announcement, coupon, or new product launch. The business makes all those the decisions and the publication runs it "as is".

When that same company embarks on a public relations campaign, and utilizes media relations and/or publicity as part of it, they basically give up control of the message. They can submit ideas, content, and news releases to a writer but in the end it is the writer and his or her editor that decides if any news on the company actually makes it into print. It is the publication that makes the decision as to when that news will run, how much of it runs, and how it might fit into the scheme of that day's news. Therefore…

Controlling the message, and how it is released, is the major difference between advertising and public relations.

Components of a PR Campaign

A Public Relations campaign can embody many facets and techniques. Some of the most common include:

- Media Relations-Publicity. This includes articles, news releases, radio/TV interviews and activities designed to result in some sort of media coverage.
- Special Events. Ground breakings, dedications, anniversary parties for clients etc.
- Contests-Competitions. Efforts to establish the best, fastest, largest, smallest, and other marks.
- Spokesperson Tour. Famous person or company spokesperson who visits numerous cities or locales to deliver the message.
- Meetings-Seminars. The exchange of information to or within a group.
- Fund Raising. An effort to raise money for charity or solicit public donations to help a non-profit organization.
- Social Responsibility Campaigns. Activities designed to engage employees and others to benefit the community.
- Coalition Building. The creation of working alliances with other groups of common interest to develop mutually beneficial programs.
- Speakers Bureau. Company employee or spokesperson delivers the message to local clubs and organizations.

- Crisis Communications. A company's response to disasters and events that could be perceived as negative by the public.

Many companies use one or more of these as part of their ongoing campaign. Other vehicles are also used to express concerns over an issue, impact targeted publics, and/or change public opinion. These vehicles include brochures, pamphlets, demonstrations, and letters to the editor, direct mail, paid ads (to support or contend a position), phone calls and signage.

Campaigns in Action

As you read this there are thousands of Public Relations campaigns in progress.

Whether realized or not, hundreds of companies are working hard to persuade you to buy their product or service. Others want to demonstrate their value to the community to perhaps earn a local tax benefit or influence politicians or voters. Still other businesses have activities in place to encourage employees to accept new wage benefits or insurance programs. Finally there are those trying to overcome scandals, product recalls, and a feeling of shakiness in the marketplace.

Some examples…

Mattel, Inc., an international toy marker finds lead paint has found its way onto thousands of products. The toys are made in China and suddenly they fear a child could become ill or even die as a result. The solution is to pull all these toys off the shelves of retailers.

Since the toy marker is a public company, they realize their stock price could fall drastically, lawsuits could ensue, and the firm's future, and that of many of its employees, may be in jeopardy.

Quickly the company springs into action. Among their PR techniques includes hosting a news conference with the CEO to announce the recall. A news tour where the CEO is interviewed on various networks. Research to trace the roots of the problem. Paid ads in selected publications signed by the CEO.

The company holds a follow-up news conference to announce they have identified the source of the problem. They make amends to change the process and spend more money on product testing. They also ask for the public's support.

Since the company maintains a large part of the toy business in the United States and elsewhere, the effects of the recall on the corporation are limited. No one has died as a result of the painting process. Network and local TV news programs do provide special segments on toys and lead paint. Parents express their concerns. Some vow to only buy toys made in America. Congress looks into new safety initiatives for exporters. Yet major damage is averted. The stock price has receded but not dwindled. Operations return to near business as usual levels.

Some of the best campaigns don't seem like campaigns at all. A case in point is Red Bull. The high energy, high octane drink became a sensation without an advertising campaign. Instead the brand used PR/event marketing techniques.

It sent out teenagers and other young people to events where college students were present. It provided samples to nearly anyone who looked like they could use an energy boost. The small can was an immediate hit. Suddenly it became the drink of choice in Silicon Valley during the Gold Rush days of the late 1990s and early 2000s. The cute little Red Bull cans started showing-up at concerts and sporting venues.

Red Bull used a word-of-mouth campaign to create thousands of product evangelists. Its Australian inventor became the richest man in his country. The brand has been expanded into 50 nations.

Many companies create a type of launch hysteria to generate interest in a new product. Often the campaign takes on a life of its own. Remember the long lines of anxious consumers waiting to purchase the first Microsoft Xbox, Talking Elmo doll, and Apple iPhone?

When hundreds if not thousands of people line-up a day or two in advance at stores nationwide to purchase the newest gadget or toy, the media will be there to cover it. Savvy public relations professionals and marketers have learned this lesson. And it seems to get repeated over and over again. While this technique has been successful it all seems to be somewhat of a spin-off of the original version of the launch of the Cabbage Patch Kids.

Remember the adoptable Cabbage Patch dolls? They were produced by a company called Coleco. About three million of these were sold in the second half of 1983, the largest introduction in the history of the toy market. The "Kids" became a part of the American culture. People spoke about them with love and appreciation. The phenomenon became much of a grass roots success story but a lot of public relations planning went into the initial launch.

Detailed thoughtfully by Jerry Hendrix in the book, *Public Relations Cases,* the public relations team spent many weeks speaking to parents, researchers, physicians, and other experts on the subject of adoption. They wanted to make sure they were sensitive to this issue before initiating the campaign. They also gained the confidence of toy retailers and many families with children prior to the holiday buying season.

Some specific techniques Coleco used included transforming their showroom at the American Toy Fair into a hospital nursery. That resulted in an article in The New York Times. In the spring, they invited various magazine editors and their children to a party where the dolls were featured at a children's museum in New York. More articles resulted. They also created a "parenting guide", embarked on a 12-city media tour, and handed out some 500,000 copies of the guide.

Coleco landed its first network television interview on the "Today" show. Then came every TV network news program. Tonight Show host Johnny Carson began talking about the dolls on a nightly basis. Articles followed in The Wall Street Journal, USA Today and dozens of newspapers. The Cabbage Patch Kids eventually showed-up on the cover of Newsweek.

The publicity created a demand for a toy that may never be equaled. Shortages occurred nationwide and eager parents paid top dollars for the dolls, if they could find one. Coleco tempered the negativity of the shortages by donating dolls to charity and working with other non-profit organizations on major events. Even Cartier placed a Cabbage Patch Kid in their window adorned with $100,000 of diamonds and emeralds, offering the doll for free with the purchase of the jewelry.

Launching Your Own Campaign

Public Relations should play a key role in the launch of any new business or to give renewed life to an existing one.

Which public relations practices you choose to put into play will be determined by several factors including your target audience, the capabilities of your staff, and your budget.

Approaches will differ for those who sell products directly to the public or consumers in general (*b to c*) vs. those businesses selling products or services to other companies (*b to b*).

Considerations must be made for whether your company can execute a campaign in-house or if it needs to hire a public relations firm. If your business has an experienced marketing/public relations professional on staff you may wish to try to develop a campaign internally. However a business lacking in PR expertise should definitely look to an agency for guidance. The right agency will have the experience and expertise necessary to develop ideas and launch the campaign.

Some factors to consider when hiring a public relations firm…

- Does the firm have experience in your product or service niche?
- Do they already work with media contacts in your industry?
- Do they have a portfolio of client work they can share with you?
- Who will service your account? (The agency owner, account executive or junior staff person)

- Are they affordable? (A smaller firm with lower hourly rates may be better suited than a larger firm charging high monthly retainer fees)
- How is your overall comfort level? (You or a staff person will be working with the firm on a regular if not daily basis. A certain bond or chemistry should be evident to make the process as engaging and enjoyable as possible.)

Most business start-ups have budget limitations. It may be necessary to start with somewhat of a limited campaign and expand as additional funds become available.

The following is a list of some campaign techniques common to new business launches…

1. **Establish Objectives.** Every campaign has a goal. Common objectives include building a brand or increasing awareness, educating prospective customers on the benefits of your product, generating product trials, etc.
2. **Write and Distribute News Releases.** Most daily newspapers and local business journals make space for articles and columns on new business launches. In order to get mentioned you'll need to send a news release to the appropriate writer or editor. Some publications will run the owner's photo along with the release. It is advised to have a professional head shot taken of the owner and perhaps other key staff. These photos can be used time and time again as opportunities present themselves. The details of how to create a news release follow in this chapter.
3. **Host an Open House.** Most new businesses host some type of launch event to let prospective customers know they exist. In many cases the businesses join their local chamber of commerce and hold an open house in conjunction with the chamber to ensure a good turnout. In some cases a ribbon cutting ceremony may be appropriate. Some businesses may wish to invite selected members of the media to attend. Others, with a large enough budget, may wish to engage a national or local celebrity to add to the festivities and to bolster publicity and awareness.

4. **Build a Solid Web Site.** In this electronic environment your web site says a lot about you and your company. After all, it is the first place most consumers visit to learn about a new company and its products. The site need not have all the latest flash technology but should be attractive with enough detail to give visitors a real flavor of your business and your expertise. It is recommend that you create some type of newsroom or place for news updates on the site. Purchase the technology that enables you to change this news and potentially other parts of the site, as events become dated.

5. **Develop a brochure and/or newsletter.** Even in this electronic world, potential customers still like to leave a business with something in their hand. A printed brochure or newsletter is useful as a tool to give to clients. If nothing else, it serves as a reminder of what they have experienced in a store, business, product demonstration or sales call. An appealing printed piece should be created that coincides with the theme of the shop or business. It need not be the most expensive artistic endeavor but one that demonstrates that the business is solid and is built to last.

6. **Attend Chamber of Commerce functions and other events.** Most start-ups have a small staff and the owner is technically identified as "the company". Therefore the owner needs to be present at a number of breakfasts, luncheons, and after hours networking events to establish their brand and build awareness. This is especially important for those in the service arena such as accountants, architects, attorneys, financial consultants, graphic designers and even public relations professionals whose names are usually etched on the door. Over time you can identify which events will bear the most return for your investment of time and money.

7. **Create a Relationship with a Local Charity.** This relationship should be a campaign or cause the owner and/or staff firmly believes in. Joining a committee, participating in a run, or supplying food or other items to a worthy organization is greatly appreciated. In many cases other committee members are likely

to do business with your company. In some cases important local decision makers are involved on the charity's board of directors and will take note of your participation, perhaps gaining an entrée for future business opportunities.

8. **Establish Relationships with Similar Businesses.** The goal here is to create a source of referrals and cross-networking with similar but not the exact same type of business. For example a health food restaurant may wish to place its brochures at a fitness center and in exchange enable the fitness center to promote its services at the restaurant. A bank may wish to place information with an insurance firm that does not offer banking services. In exchange, the insurance firm could host seminars on the bank's premises and invite a number of their selected clients to attend, thus exposing potential new customers to the bank's facilities. A new graphic design firm may wish to host a luncheon for area advertising and PR agencies. The end game is to build your own list of customers as you help others do the same.
9. **"Influence The Influencers".** This technique is designed to get some of the major influencers in your community to talk about your product and act as evangelists for your company. Often called a word-of-mouth campaign, this has been a staple with high-tech firms launching new computers and related devices. Key leaders and members of the media are often the first to get a new product before it becomes available to the general public. Restaurants often have a VIP type opening night inviting selected dignitaries to sample their food. The same concept can be used for start-ups and others selling new products for consumer and/or business use.
10. **Develop a List of Customer Testimonials.** As new customers come on board it is a strong advantage to elicit testimonials from them. If a well known person or representative from a top local company samples your product and likes it, ask for permission to use their name on your web site and other marketing materials. Many restaurants place photos of celebrities on their walls who have dined at their establishment. The concept can be used for

other businesses as well. A few of these will help to immediately establish your company's credibility as a solid competitor in your industry.

Creating the News Release

The news release is the fulcrum for any business wishing to generate publicity for their company.

Reporters and editors will not respond to a story proposal without some type of printed document. The news release or press release is the most accepted form of delivering news to the media.

The most important thing to remember about the release is the word "news". There must be some news value or the piece is not worth writing.

Some discussion can be initiated between public relations professionals as to the look and feel of the release but generally all releases adhere to a standard format.

The document on the adjoining page will give you a good example of how it should look.

The release should include the following information…

1. The city or location of the origination of the document.
2. The date of distribution.
3. A headline written in bold type.
4. A leading stand-alone paragraph with enough information that the reader can get the basics of the story without having to scroll downward.
5. A second paragraph adding more detail.
6. A third paragraph, usually a quote from the owner or president of the company.

7. A fourth paragraph that talks briefly about the company and how consumers can contact it via phone and web site.
8. A media contact reporters can call for questions or additional information.
9. A designation symbolizing the release is over. Either "30" or ### are acceptable

Some companies prefer to use a double space between sentences; others use single space between lines. This writer prefers single spacing especially since nearly all releases are emailed, providing a reporter with a quick read.

In nearly all cases the release should be kept to just one page. Most reporters will tell you if you can't get it all in one page it's probably not worth reading. This is especially true when pitching story ideas to television and radio news producers and editors.

It is also advisable to paste the news release into the body of the email. Many newspapers and other outlets look to attachments as possible e-mail scam. Some are blocked by firewalls. Others get totally deleted.

Keep in mind reporters get dozens if not hundreds of emails per day. Depending on the likes and dislikes of the writer it is usually a sound practice to call a reporter either before you send the release (informing them you are sending them some important new information so they will keep a watch for it) or after you send it to make sure they received it. In the fast paced deadline oriented news business, releases are easily lost in the shuffle or simply forgotten despite promising story potential.

Media Contact:	John Smith, Smith's Fine Steaks 212-555-5555 jsmith@smithssteaks.com

Smith's Fine Steaks to Open in Tortuga Valley

TORTUGA VALLEY, NY -- November 1, 2008 -- John Smith, the highly noted and award winning restaurateur, announces the opening of Smith's Fine Steaks, Saturday, November 8, 2008, 5pm, at 500

Main Street in Tortuga Valley. The restaurant is Smith's first eatery in the area and will feature a variety of delicacies including prime cuts of beef, Alaskan salmon, other fresh varieties of sea food, and an extensive wine list.

Smith is the owner of Alfredo's Italian Dinery in Central Islip and John's Steak House in Albany. His award winning cuisine has been featured in national magazines such as Bonne Appetite, Food and Wine, and Gourmet, as well as local publications including the New York Times, and the New York Daily News.

"We are pleased to make Tortuga Valley the home of our new concept in fine dining," Smith said. "Local diners will enjoy our prime rib, filets, and a great selection of the freshest fish. The facility itself is entirely state-of-the-art with one of the largest kitchens in the area. The entire Smith family looks forward to a long and successful relationship serving the Tortuga Valley community."

About Smith's Fine Steaks

The Smith name has been associated with fine dining since 1960. John Smith is the third generation of his family to operate his own restaurant. Smith's Fine Steaks is the family's latest concept in dining with over 10,000 square feet and the ability to serve 200 diners as well as host parties and special events. Hours are 11am to 10pm Tuesday through Thursday, 11am to 11pm Friday and Saturday, and 11am to 8pm on Sundays. Reservations are recommended. For additional information visit www.smithssteaks.com or call 212-555-5555.

Social Media and PR

Any discussion of public relations must include "social media". Social media usually means sites built on self-generated content. In other words writings, audio and video posted straight from the creator onto an online gathering place.

These gathering places include such well-known sites as Facebook, My Space, and You Tube. Also in the mix are 3D virtual sites such as

Second Life. Social outlets continue to grow in popularity but should you use them as part of your campaign?

The answer is probably not. Most businesses are better off investing their limited dollars, and limited time, into traditional media. Articles in newspapers and magazines, as well as community events, and other tactics, will produce a bigger "bang for the buck' than trying to chat-up a group of young adults on a social site or placing a corporate sponsored video on You Tube.

That being said, a nightclub, music store or clothing shop appealing to teens might be a good candidate for some type of exposure on a social site. A chain of stores might also engage in community building. In other words maintaining an area where customers can talk to store executives and exchange ideas or even talk amongst themselves. The goal is to create some evangelists for your company as you endear customers to your business. You might offer online specials, maintain a birthday club, or even create some coupons to be sent periodically to the customer's email address.

As this book goes to press, many corporations continue to experiment with social media. It will be of interest to determine if any value can be realized from these efforts over the long term.

(1) Effective Public Relations, 6th Edition. 1985. Prentice-Hall, Inc.

CHAPTER 9
TV AND PUBLICITY

What Is Publicity?

Okay you know what business you want to start or maybe you're already in business; customers and cash flow are the lifelines of your business. And even though you have a few loyal clients you'd like to attract new customers. So how do you do it, how do you give your business a boost? Media exposure and Publicity could be the key.

Okay first let's define Publicity... Publicity is the attempt to manage the public's perception of a subject. This includes people, goods, services, organizations and works of arts or entertainment. (Wikipedia)

From a marketing perspective publicity is one component of promotion and the ultimate goal is to promote the client's product or services. Publicity is information disseminated to attract public notice; this would be in the form of a story aired or article written about your business or product and although it is not a commercial it can be just as effective in attracting attention and new business.

Some would even argue that publicity carries more credibility than advertising (commercials). The assumption is either you have attracted the media's attention because you have a good product or that you have done something good. Now before we dive into making our business a prime target for publicity, lets first consider the different types of media.

Types Of Media

First let's look at Print media... this consists of newspapers, magazines and other published materials. This medium can reach local, regional, national and sometimes international audiences. The advantages of this media is it's mobile and transferable; you can take a magazine or newspaper anywhere and when you are finished you can pass it on to someone else. And if you are searching for a previously published story or article that ran days, months even years earlier you can find it at your local library and sometimes online.

Now we're going to look at Broadcast media, this consists of Radio and Television outlets. Like print, broadcast media can also reach local, regional, national and sometimes international audiences. While print materials are transferable and have a wide reach, some local television and radio stations have signals that are limited to certain areas. However certain Broadcast outlets have national and international reach. If you have created a product or run a business and you're looking to attract clients from all over the country your approach may be a little different than those looking for clients on a local or regional level. If you are marketing your services or products to clients locally, you would shoot for local and regional exposure. If your services and products are available across the country; national exposure would be beneficial to you.

Advertising Costs

There are also different types of media exposure; one way to get exposure is from Television commercials or Ads (short for advertising), another option is Publicity.

First let's look at commercials…Commercials are pre produced ads with actors, scripts and all the bells and whistles. Commercials can be produced by the marketing/production department at a television or radio station, or a production company or advertising agency can get the job done. With advertising you will also pay for a particular time slot or space where your commercial or ad will be run for a set number of times. The upside is your business will get exposure, the downside it's going to cost you.

Now let's look at some costs to produce various radio and television commercials and run ads in the newspaper. (These quotes are estimates gathered from various sources and media outlets).

Producing National Television Commercials

The cost to produce a 30 second National television spot can National TV spots can run anywhere from $3,000 to $400,000. If you shop around, a local video production company may be able to get it done for less than a thousand dollars.

Producing Local Television Commercials

The cost to produce a local television commercial can run anywhere from a few hundred to several thousand dollars. When producing a local television commercial there are many factors to consider… Are you going with a production company or the production department of a television station? Will it be shot on location or in the studio? Can you save money by using recycled commercials or pre-packaged ads? The bottom line is the more you do your homework and shop around the more likely you are to cut your costs.

Remember the cost to produce a television commercial doesn't cover the cost to run the ad, that price can vary based on the time and frequency that your ad will air.

Producing Local Radio Commercials

Radio is more reasonable when it comes to advertising. The key to remember is who your target audience is and does this station reach listeners who are potential customers or clients. If you choose to run your ad on a particular radio station their on-air talent and production department can usually produce your commercial in house. You will have to pay for it to run on the station which can cost you anywhere between One hundred to five hundred dollars or more depending on the time and how often your commercial airs. You can minimize your cost and maximize your exposure with buying advertising packages; stations will sell you several commercials that will run at different times of the day that will run for weeks or months.

National Newspaper Ads

Here are some figures of what it would cost you to run an ad in a national newspaper Full-page black and white and color ads in a national paper can run you between $100,000 to $200,000. A half page ad will cost you around $95,000.

Local Newspaper Ads

If you want to run a full page ad in your local paper it can run anywhere from $1000 dollars to $15,000. If you live in a smaller community the more reasonable the cost, the larger the city the higher the price.

Now if you're just getting started you probably don't have the budget to pay for an agency to produce commercials for your business and buy airtime for advertising radio or television stations. So how do you get exposure without breaking the bank? Publicity, and there are several ways to attract the media's attention that could ultimately attract new clients.

We talked about print and broadcast media but we are going to focus on the most powerful medium of influence; television. And although television is our target for the following strategies explained later in this chapter they apply to all media including radio and print.

In the previous chapters you learned how the press release can aid in the process of promoting your business. It can introduce the media to your company or business and inform them of any changes in your services. But before you make that mad dash to the mailbox to send off that press release find out who you need to send your press release to and why._

Know Your Newscasts and Your Newsroom

Most local television stations have at least four newscasts... the morning, the midday and two evening newscasts. These do not include the national newscasts. There are similarities and differences in the formats, for example most newscasts lead with "hard news" (crime etc.) whereas the "softer news" (feature stories) is routinely placed toward the middle or end of the newscast. The evening and midday newscasts are typically 30 minutes long including commercials. The morning newscasts are usually longer and can run anywhere from an hour to two hours running news and other segments in a two hour loop. The logical conclusion is longer newscast means a better chance of getting on the show. This does not mean that you can't get on a midday or evening show; it just means you are working with less time and opportunity.

Most morning shows have more time for interviews, feature segments and human interest stories. If you are planning something and you are looking for coverage it also helps to know who to contact. Call the station(s) and ask for the name of the Morning producer or assignment editor and forward your materials to target someone in charge of deciding what will be covered. I have received lots of packets, invitations, press releases addressed to me personally; don't be afraid to follow up with a call to make sure your information was received even if you have to leave a voice message. Before you send the producer or assignment editor a press release think about what's the catchiest or interesting aspect about the your product or services, and highlight these key points in your press packet or conversation.

Now that you know a little bit more about newscasts and who to contact in the newsroom lets develop some strategies to get publicity. The following are some ways to attract the Media's attention. I like to call them "Paths to Publicity"

Freebies/Demonstrations

You have services to offer or a stockroom full of inventory, how do you move it from the storeroom into the customer's hands? In some cases you have to give something to get something, and this can also hold true when you're looking to increase your company's visibility. Let's take a simple trip to the grocery store. You've already decided what you need, and you've made a list.

Milk Eggs Butter Cereal

You get to the store and you're headed for the dairy products for the butter and milk and then you see her, yes the lady with the toothpick and the treat on the end of it. And you are drawn to her display like ants to a picnic. Why? Because whatever's on that toothpick you already know it's free. It could be barbecued buffalo meat but you're standing there patiently waiting for your FREE sample. You want to test the theory. Let's imagine the same scenario but when you approach the display the person says that will be one dollar to sample this product. You would lose interest, maybe offended. Why? "Free" grabs your attention every time. Do you have a Grand Opening, new product or contest that you want to promote? Don't be afraid to include samples in your media kit when you contact the press.

If you have a new product or have come up with the recipe for the best donuts in town, don't hesitate to send a dozen to the newsroom along with your press release. Or if you design jewelry from recycled materials, don't be afraid to send a pair of earrings to the morning producer with details of what makes your product different. Send an invitation to the morning producer and anchor. Remember try to find something unique or new about your product, business or about yourself or why you started your business. I am not advocating giving away products or services that would jeopardize your business's profits. What I am saying is don't be afraid to offer samples or demonstrations that will showcase your business and introduce what you have to offer to potential new clients.

Another element of "freebies" is a contest or giveaway. Okay let's say you run a Lawn Care or Landscaping business. Contact your local media and inquire about how you can participate in a contest or giveaway by offering your services. It's May and you offer to give one lucky family a backyard makeover for the viewer to be announced on the Midday Newscast. Every day for 2 weeks the television station is announcing this contest as they encourage viewers to register. What's in it for you? Every day the name of your business is being announced over and over. This sparks an interest in viewers who had never heard of your business before, and now viewers are hitting your website because their lawns are in desperate need of care. Now maybe you can take some before and after photos of lawn of the lucky contest winner and show them during the newscast. This is a free commercial and promotion and well worth doing one backyard for free. Check with your local television station and see if you can partner with them on this win/win proposition.

Will this approach work? I produced a Morning newscast and scheduled a variety of guests and companies. On several occasions I received correspondence from previous guests thanking me for having them on the show and explaining how the exposure brought in new clientele. Volunteer to come on the show and demonstrate how your restaurant prepares foods that are healthy, bring in some of the entrees and let the crew sample them on the air. From time to time a car dealership will hold a contest to give away a car to whoever can stay awake the longest while keeping their hands on the car. And these contests attract the media's attention every time. You see those sleep deprived, caffeine consuming contestants barely standing trying to maintain contact with the car ultimately roll away with the new set of wheels. Some radio stations often do live remotes on location from dealership. Throughout the contest the announcer repeats the name and the location of the business that that they are broadcasting live from. So who's the real winner? Now you've got the picture.

Creativity

Journalists travel the world to cover news and current events. And while the saying "There's nothing new under the sun" may not be completely true sometimes it seems that way to the reporters and producers who have seen astonishing sights and met remarkable people. Consequently people flock to what's new, what's unusual and sometimes bizarre. Am I advocating stretching the truth or doing something out of character to get the media's attention? Absolutely not, what I am saying is accentuate or focus on what's interesting and unique about your business or yourself. Are you the owner of a music shop that gives free lessons to underprivileged kids?

Are you a chef who creates edible napkin rings and centerpieces? Is there a unique reason why you started your business, did you overcome incredible odds to start your business? Have you put a new twist on an old idea? It's like the car dealership that has someone dressed in a guerilla suit with the sign. Do they really think you would buy a car from someone dressed up a guerilla suit? Nope, they are just trying to get your attention. You see cars every day, all day. But a guerilla probably will catch your eye. There was a man who dressed in various costumes and marched up and down the street with his baton. He has attracted the attention of the local and national media. Why? Because he was notably different and he spent his time doing something that we normally don't see.

Piggyback/Tie Ins

Another way to gain exposure for your business is through piggybacking or tie-ins. Let's look at the concept of piggybacking. Well as a child you might remember the piggyback ride, you jump on someone else's back and they take you where you want to go (hopefully). The key is you are traveling via someone else's efforts and you are just going along for the ride. The concept is similar when dealing with publicity; you can piggyback off of a national or local story. For example, let's say there is a problem with the national beef supply. Now you're a local restaurateur and you've owned The Barnyard Chicken Shack for years but since the beef scare you can't keep the chicken sandwiches coming fast enough. Is this a coincidence? Are the two factors related? You don't have to do any intense research, contact the local media and let them know how fast chicken sandwiches are flying off the grill, more exposure and customers for you.

Sometimes holidays provide tie-in opportunities for certain businesses, but you have to create these opportunities and give the media enough time to say yes and fit you into their schedule or lineup. Here's the scenario it's December 27th, Christmas is over. Folks have shopped till they dropped racked up monumental credit card charges at the before and after Holiday sales, waited in lines to return itchy sweaters and other unwanted gifts. And to top it everyone is complaining about how many pounds they have packed on at those the Holiday parties. And like clockwork the media is doing stories on the Post Holiday depression.

Now let's say you are the owner of a spa or a gym. I would contact the media and let them know that you are running a special beat the post holiday blues special and how this would make a wonderful gift to yourself or a loved one. Also put a special twist on it, tell folks who come to join the gym or visit the spa to bring in an unwanted gift and you will take a certain amount off of the visit or membership and donate the items to those less fortunate next year. Ideally you could have a crew come to the gym to see what services you offer, but you could also come to the station and showcase some of your services that you offer. For example if you give massages you could show someone getting a neck massage or facial. A good attention grabber would be to explain how much exercise it would take to burn off those pounds that were packed on during the holidays. Have someone in the studio doing repetitions of various exercises.

The spa and gym idea can also be a draw on Valentine's Day; it's not just for florists and confectioners. If couples are trying to win the "Battle of the Bulge" a box of chocolates may be an unwelcome sight on Valentine's Day. As the owner of a gym whip up special pages deal in honor of the holiday. You can offer a two for one special for couples. Invite a news crew to a walkthrough of the facility before or close to the holiday, have the reporter tryout the equipment, top it off with a trip to the massage chair and watch your business boom.

Collaboration

Collaboration with another business or company for a special event or campaign is another way to attract the media's attention. Just imagine for a moment if the two major soft drink companies joined forces to create "The Ultimate Soft Drink"?

It would create media frenzy, definitely make headlines. Now realistically we will we probably never see that business venture in our lifetime, but there are some entities that have come together, sometimes temporarily for a project or promotion that attracted the media and the public's interest. In 2006 during the baseball season one of the food vendors at the stadium in St. Louis were serving hamburgers to local fans, the twist…, the hamburger patties were sandwiched between Krispy Krème Donuts. The local media jumped on it, was this oddly paired duo a delicious treat? I don't know, but the media attention sparked my curiosity and had I been in the area I would have tried the unique combo. Another story of collaboration drew the media's attention a local jeweler has joined forces with a Confectionery or Candy Shop to create the ultimate gift…diamonds and chocolates. What captured the media's attention is the novelty of two elements that you normally don't find together in one neat package. So if you can collaborate for a special date or event. Try it, the sky is the limit.

Lending Your Expertise

Sometimes we see "experts" discussing a subject on television and think, I could never do that, I don't know enough, and I'm not smart enough. Wrong. Let's say you run a tax preparation service and there have been major changes in the forms of the upcoming year. You should immediately be thinking about contacting your local news organizations and volunteering to come on and talk about these changes. Because people will take down your name and number to avoid the headaches come April 15th. You've donated a little time, increased your visibility and attracted new clients. Most opportunities won't knock on your door, you have to create them. One day I picked up a local newspaper and an article caught my eye. There was a radio special scheduled dealing with the issue of aging parents. I had a client who specialized in eldercare placement and care. I informed her that she should consider trying to get on the show. I called the radio station and told them about my client was an expert in this subject.

They informed me that they were already booked for the segment. I continued to inform them of her credentials and offered to fax over her information. After they received her information they were impressed with her expertise and agreed to interview her, the interview was aired on the radio station and her business was brought into the spotlight via the interview. Months later the same radio station contacted her to do another interview for another series that they were producing.

What keeps someone from lending their expertise? Lack of confidence in their knowledge of their subject or field, simply put…second guessing themselves. What most people should know is if you own a business or company, your knowledge of a related subject is probably greater than the general public and gives you the credibility sufficient to do an interview about the topic. Now there are times when only an "expert" will do. You've heard of the FAA (Federal Aviation Administration) the FDA (Food and Drug Administration) FEMA (Federal Emergency Management Administration), when there is a major crises or disaster there are times when notable experts are needed to walk us through the incident and impending events. But there are times when your expertise will suffice. How does lending your expertise help you? Doing interviews increases your visibility, adds to your credibility and possibly introduces you to potential clients could use your services. Most stations have websites so viewers can look at the story again and possibly link to your website and services. So don't underestimate yourself or your credentials and keep yourself up to date on your field or your business

Good Deeds

There seems to be a mission by local television stations to report more "good news". I guess viewers are tired of seeing "bad news". Local stations are running promotions asking the public to contact them and report the "good things" going on in their neighborhoods, local heroes or kids who are doing good things, and the list goes on and on. What does that mean for you and your business? I am not advocating "staging" an event to attract media attention or flying around like Robin Hood or a Superhero in hopes that the local media will come knocking at your door. What I am saying is businesses and individuals have inadvertently received media attention by reaching out and helping someone in need. And if you or your business is planning something to help the community, give the media a heads up on the event.

There was a young boy whose identity will remain anonymous was kidnapped and found. A homebuilding company came forward to remodel or rebuild the family's home; a local dealership also donated a truck to a teen that helped provide vital information in the case. If someone were in the market to buy or build a home or a vehicle these two companies might have an edge on the competition, because their good deed thrust them into the spotlight and oftentimes we associate good deeds with good standards. Is this necessarily an accurate assumption? I don't know, it's just how it works sometimes.

You may be thinking I can't do something on that scale I'm just a hair stylist that works in someone else's shop. Okay take this scenario you have a family that just lost everything in a fire, no one was hurt. There is a teenager who will not be attending her Senior Prom because her parent's priorities are getting a place to live and replacing the things that were lost. So what can you do? You can volunteer to do her hair for free, and then the nail tech says she'll throw in a free manicure and pedicure. You contact the local department store and they say she can come in to pick out a dress. It's not a farfetched idea... I've gotten department stores to donate clothes for a "Back to School" fashion show, no questions asked. And a local florist and limousine service might pitch in too.

And there you have it, this family who has suffered a loss will have a little to smile about a teen won't have to miss a once in a lifetime event and you better believe the media wouldn't miss this story either.

Good deeds can also come in the form of providing an opportunity for others. For example you can offer internships to underprivileged youths; you can take donations for those in need. Don't do a good deed for the attention but if you're going to reach out to your community, let the media know about it

Timing Is Everthing

No matter what path to publicity you take remember "timing is everything" in the news business. Sometimes you hit home run, sometimes you'll strike out, but don't throw in the towel. Earlier in the chapter I told you about the client who was an Eldercare specialist who was invited to be a guest on a local radio station. In a quest to keep her business in the spotlight we devised a plan to promote her business in conjunction with Grandparents Day. We decided to use the holiday to address eldercare issues and explore many aspects of caring for the aged. We had care, gifts, and family issues covered. The curveball... that year Grandparent's Day fell on the anniversary of September 11th. · And as expected the media and public would be consumed by this solemn anniversary.

Each year Grandparent's Day falls pretty close to this date. Now that we know how the two events overlap we are aware of the hurdles that we face. However sometimes obstacles are unforeseen. I had client who was planning and anticipating the grand opening of a Community Rehabilitation and Training center. I'd contacted the local media, sent press releases and was prepared to ask for a provisional commitment of some type of coverage of this event. Well the night before the community center was set to open, our baseball team The St. Louis Cardinals won the World Series. Well there would be no coverage of the grand opening of the Community and Training Center. There was no need to contact the media; most things were taking a back seat to non-stop World Series coverage.

A vacant building in an area plagued by gangs and other problems had been transformed into a training and rehabilitation center, this was newsworthy, but it was a good story at the wrong time. What's the solution? Sometimes you can rework a missed opportunity. Here are a few suggestions if your "Big Event" happens to coincide with an event of major proportions, set an "anniversary celebration", hold a contest, or if there is a new addition to the business i.e. building, service etc. let the media and the public know about it. Try to send your press release and media kit well in advance of the event so a producer can work you into a show or newscast.

If you are releasing a book or publication remember most broadcast publicity is centered on the book's publication date. If you send a newsletter about your new swimsuit line while folks are still shoveling snow out of their driveways you probably won't get a call. Producers work on tight deadlines on a daily basis. Sometimes no means not right now; wrong day, wrong season or it could be a heavy news days with lots of breaking news. Follow up with phone calls, be persistent, but don't be a pest. And remember timing is everything in this business.

The Right Place at the Right Time

We've discussed several ways to seek out the media with hopes of getting their attention and publicity, but there are times when the media will come to you; well sort of. You can anticipate the media's moves. Sometimes businesses owners don't have to go searching out the media sometimes the media comes to them. How many times a snowstorm hit a town and news crew has goes hunting for the store that still has salt and shovels. Sometimes your business can be in the right place at the right time.

Every year there are certain events that the media covers like clockwork. As a reporter I remember covering the same events year after year. Sometimes as I was heading to the event it was like déjà vu. For your town it may be a fair or a festival. "The Taste of … insert your city's name) " has become a popular summer event with the public and the media. Most times where there is a crowd, a good cause and good food…the news crews are there. So you've got best barbecue sauce and ribs in town. You might consider renting a booth at your hometown's fairs and festivals. And when your lookout spots the news media pulling up I'd be waiting for them with food in hand. Don't be shy; that's why they are there to cover the event, and wouldn't it be nice if they set up right in front of your table telling the folks back at the studio and thousands of viewers that your ribs are worth coming to the festival for. The media has a powerful and instantaneous impact on our perception of a product or business.

Recently one of the networks did a taste test of sorbets, and one brand got rave reviews. The next time I went grocery shopping I went on a quest to find this frosty treat. Now this item was not on my grocery list, but the media coverage had seared the images and description of this product into my memory bank. Never underestimate the power of the media and its impact on perception and power to influence buying trends._

Be Prepared And Practice

If you are chosen to prepare a five course dinner for ten guests I wouldn't advise you to wait an hour before their arrival to start preparing the meal. The same hold true for establishing and building an alliance with the media and clients. Keeps information regarding your company or business current? Wouldn't it be a shame if you faxed over a press release with a phone number that was changed a year ago; no wonder that producer didn't call. Here's an incident that happened to me. I was sending press releases to media outlets for a client, and I was almost done, down to the last three stations when I realized all of the pages I had previously faxed were blank.

I know you're thinking wow she doesn't know how to use a fax machine. Well in my defense I had just replaced my fax machine and the old machine faxed with the pages down and this one was pages up. I had twenty minutes before I had to head out the door and I had to refax all those press releases. The point is prepare ahead of time and test out things before crunch time. As well as keeping your information current about your business, make sure the contacts and phone number in your rolodex are current, sometimes people leave or change departments or positions. So take a few minutes and call the main number to the station and update your list of contacts

Parting Words of Advice

Find out who your target consumer is and what form of media they listen to or watch. If you have created and are marketing a trendy clothing line for teenagers your clients more than likely won't be listening to News or Talk radio. Do some research find out what show would be suit your needs

Never send a "blind package" (unaddressed) to a newsroom, it might end up in the trash or be hauled away by security. Stations receive numerous parcels and letters on a daily basis. Some are resumes from recent graduates looking for their big break; some of it is junk mail. Don't let your materials get lost in the shuffle; get a name so that your packet will reach its intended target.

Practice does make perfect… talk about your business and focus on what makes it unique. Practice in the mirror, to the cat, to anyone who will listen. It will help during interviews, but it will also help when selling your product or services to potential clients.

Printed in the United States
118919LV00005B/19/P

9 781434 361530